MW00355679

THE BAKER CHOCOLATE company

Looking east from Eliot Street in Milton Village, the Pierce Mill can be seen in the center distance, with wood mills along both sides of the Neponset River. *Courtesy of Earl Taylor.*

THE BAKER CHOCOLATE COMPANY

A SWEET HISTORY

ANTHONY M. SAMMARCO

THE
History
PRESS

Published by The History Press
Charleston, SC 29403
www.historypress.net

First published 2009
Second printing 2009

ISBN 978.1.5402.1819.3

Library of Congress Cataloging-in-Publication Data

Sammarco, Anthony Mitchell.
The Baker Chocolate Company : a sweet history / Anthony Sammarco.
p. cm.
Includes bibliographical references.
ISBN 978-1-5402-1819-3
1. Baker Chocolate Company (Dorchester (Boston, Mass.)) 2. Chocolate industry-
-Massachusetts--Boston--Dorcester--History. 3. Businesspeople--United States--
Biography. I. Title.
HD9200.U54.B357 2009
338.7'6645--dc22
2009033691

CONTENTS

ACKNOWLEDGEMENTS

C hocolate is a mysterious yet sublimely delicious substance. It was a drink before it became a delicacy, a food before it became a delicious treat.

There have been many people who assisted me in the research and writing of this book on "a very delicious memory from the past"; however, I would like to especially thank Andy Sawicky for sharing his time, expertise, knowledge and, with the loan of some interesting advertisements, pieces of ephemera and photographs from his collection of Baker Chocolate memorabilia used in this book. I would also like to thank Anne Flanagan Thompson for the use of her research material, conversations and sharing her unbounded enthusiasm for "all things Baker." Without the assistance, immense patience and unflagging support of Cesidio "Joe" Cedrone, this book would never have been completed, and I dedicate this book to him.

I would also like to offer sincere thanks to Donald and Cynthia Agnetta; the residents of Baker Square Condominiums; Donald Blair; the Boston Public Library, Print Room, Aaron Schmidt; Helen Buchanan; the late Paul G. Buchanan; Judith Reed Emmons Bullock; Sean Cahill; Mary Jo Campbell; Cedar Grove Cemetery; the late Donato Cedrone-Sammarco; Elise Ciregna and Stephen LoPiccolo; Edith G. Clifford; Regina Clifton; Elizabeth Curtiss; the Dallas, Texas Public Library, Rachel Garrett Howell; William Dillon; the Dorchester Community News; Mike Doyle; Jean Dudley; Olivia Grant Dybing; the marvelous world of eBay; the late Dr. Lydia Bowman Edwards; the late A. Bradlee Emmons; the late Joan Estelle Evans; William Fall; Robert Fitzgerald; Captain Forbes House Museum, Christine Sullivan, director; Russell Fox; Jean Goldman and Vincent DaForno; Edward Gordon; Helen Hannon; Historic Burying Ground Initiative, city of Boston; Historic New England, Lorna Condon; James

Hobin; Chuck and Pam Huckins; Hutchinson; Peter Jackson and Donna Dickerson; Stephen Kharfen; James Z. Kyprianos; Nadine Leary; Jane S. Lemire; Tim Lemire; Paul Leo; Joseph LoPiccolo; Judith McGillicuddy; Karen L. Mac Nutt Esq.; Milton Cemetery, Therese Desmond Sills; Mittens; Mount Auburn Cemetery, Janet Hayward; Frank Norton; Ellen Ochs; Stephen O'Donnell; Susan W. Paine; the late Stephen Davies Paine; James Pardy; Frances Perkins and Charlie Rosenberg; Jeannette Lithgow Peverly; Loretta Philbrook; Mark Pickering; Museum of Fine Arts, Boston, Erin Schleigh; Linda Mason Pirie, president of the Milton Historical Society; Steven Pirie; Elva Proctor; Lilian M.C. Randall; Kita Reece; Margaret Recanzone; Saunders Robinson, my editor; Nina and Anthony Salvucci; Carolyn Savage; Robert Bayard Severy; Staatliche Kunstsammlungen, Dresden, Germany, Yvonne Brandt; Jeanne Sutton; Earl Taylor, president of the Dorchester Historical Society; Anne and George Thompson; Carolyn D. Thornton; Archives and Special Collections, Healey Library, University of Massachusetts Boston, Elizabeth Mock; the Urban College of Boston; Peter Van Delft; the Victorian Society, New England Chapter; Steven Walker, South End Photo Lab; Ann and Thomas Walsh; *Wikipedia*, the Free Encyclopedia; the late Marion White Woodbridge; Monica Woodbridge; Virginia M. White; and James Preston Wysong.

However, per the specific request of Mary A. Carragher Esq., attorney for Kraft Foods, the successor in interest to the Walter Baker Chocolate Company and owner of the Baker's Chocolate trademark and La Belle Chocolatiere design trademark, Kraft Foods wished to state that it "does not authorize, endorse or sponsor this book and was in no way affiliated with it." Nor did they offer any cooperation or assistance.

INTRODUCTION

If the Chocolate does not prove good, the Money will be returned.

The Lower Mills, known by the Neponset Tribe of the Massachusetts Indians as *Unquety*, meaning "Lower Falls" in Algonquin, is in Dorchester, Massachusetts, and is the site of the first gristmill in New England (1634), the first powder mill in New England (1665), the first iron slitting mill (1710), the first paper mill in New England (1728), the first chocolate mill in America (1765), the first folio and quarto letter paper in New England (1803) and the first power-sawn veneers in America (1817). By the time of the Civil War, the Lower Mills, which encompasses the towns of Dorchester and Milton, Massachusetts, but is known as Milton Village south of the Neponset River, was made up of commercial concerns that once employed close to one thousand people. There were once four independent chocolate manufacturers in the Lower Mills, with the Baker, Preston, Dr. Jonathan Ware and Webb & Twombley Chocolate Companies producing so much chocolate that the pervasive and heady aroma led to the area being called "Chocolate Village." Though a few of the commercial concerns continued into the twentieth century, by 1881, the competitive chocolate manufacturers were all to be absorbed by the Baker Chocolate Company, the oldest manufacturer of chocolate in this country. Chocolate was one of the most deliciously prolific, as well as profitable, concerns developed since the introduction of the cacao to the colonies in the mid-eighteenth century.

In 1765, as tradition has it, Dr. James Baker (1739–1825) of Dorchester met John Hannon, "a penniless Irish immigrant," crying on the banks of the Neponset River. Inquiring as to his obvious distress, Baker learned that

The Neponset River, named for the Native American tribe of Massachusetts Indians, was harnessed as early as 1634 for water power. Over the next two centuries, many mills, such as grist, gunpowder and paper, were erected along the river, including the Baker Chocolate Mills.

Hannon was destitute but that he possessed the skill of making chocolate, having learned it in England. As chocolate and cocoa were not only delicious commodities but also fashionable extravagances imported from Europe, Baker financially backed Hannon in a leased, small, wood-framed mill in Milton Village, where "Hannon's Best Chocolate" was manufactured for almost fifteen years, with an incredible guaranteed money-back policy that stated, "If the Chocolate does not prove good, the Money will be returned." In 1779, Hannon is said to have sailed to the West Indies, according to the town history, to purchase cacao beans, but the ungallant rumor was that he deserted his shrewlike wife, Elizabeth Gore Hannon. Whatever his reason for leaving, he never returned. After hiring Nathaniel Blake to carry on the chocolate business, a year after her husband's departure, the "Widow" Hannon, who was remarried in 1782 to William Walker, sold her share of the enterprise to Dr. James Baker, who established the Baker Chocolate Company in 1780.

Edmund Baker (1770–1846), the son of Dr. James and Lydia Bowman Baker, and later Colonel Walter Baker (1792–1852), the son of Edmund and Sarah Howe Baker, entered the family business and continued the family tradition of manufacturing chocolate and marketing it as being as "absolutely pure as it is soluble," with a guaranteed money-back policy if one

Dr. James Baker (1739–1825) was to provide financial backing for John Hannon, who made chocolate in a rented mill for fourteen years. In 1780, after Hannon disappeared, Dr. Baker established Baker Chocolate, which was continued by his son and grandson until 1852.

was not absolutely satisfied for any reason with the product. During the early years of the Victorian period, Walter Baker, who was educated at Harvard College (class of 1818) like his father and grandfather before him, entered the family business after having studied law with Judge Tappan Reeve in Litchfield, Connecticut. Therefore, Baker was not only able to continue the family's lucrative production of chocolate, but he was also able to legally protect its name and trademark from infringement on the name "Baker's" by his numerous and sundry competitors. Walter Baker's success was evident. In 1839, he donated the funds to build Lyceum Hall on Dorchester's Meeting House Hill, declining the honor of having it named for him, and in 1852, he generously donated an impressive four-sided spire clock to the Second Church in Codman Square in Dorchester, Massachusetts, of which he was a member.

Following the untimely death of Walter Baker in 1852, and the subsequent death of his brother-in-law, Sidney Williams, two years later, Henry Lillie Pierce (1825–1896), a stepnephew of Walter Baker, was allowed to lease the chocolate mill at the Lower Mills, paying to the trustees of the Baker Estate a fairly substantial sum to lease the business over the next three decades. Henry Lillie Pierce, once a three-dollars-per-week clerk in the Baker Chocolate Company countinghouse prior to 1854, began to plan long-range goals to expand the chocolate mill in its physical size, as well as to market his delicious product throughout the country. Henry Lillie Pierce was said to be an honest and just man, and having once worked at Baker's as a trusted employee, he was possibly more inclined to treat his employees fairly when he assumed overall control of the business. During the post–Civil War years, Pierce began to enter the chocolate and cocoa produced by his employees in various competitive expositions, and the chocolate was to receive the

Henry Lillie Pierce (1825–1896) was president of Walter Baker & Company from 1854 until his death. He increased the cocoa and chocolate business fortyfold and was a well-respected businessman and political leader.

highest awards in 1873 at the Vienna Exhibition in Germany and in 1876 at the Philadelphia Centennial Exhibition held in honor of the 100th anniversary of the United States of America. Pierce was to adopt La Belle Chocolatiere as his trademark in 1881, having seen the pastel portrait *Das Schokoladenmadchen* by the Swiss painter Jean-Etienne Liotard at the Dresden Art Gallery in Germany. He promptly renamed it *La Belle Chocolatiere* and formally adopted the chocolate server as his registered trademark in 1883; subsequently, it became synonymous with the oldest manufacturer of chocolate in the ensuing years.

After the town of Dorchester, Massachusetts, was annexed to the city of Boston on January 4, 1870, Pierce was to serve as mayor of the city in 1872 and 1877, as well as a member of the Massachusetts House of Representatives in 1861, 1862 and 1866 and as a United States congressman between 1873 and 1877. In 1895, nine years after the incorporation of the company, and nine years after Pierce was allowed to purchase the company from the trustees of the Baker Estate, Pierce said to his secretary, "The die is cast. Walter Baker & Company is now a corporate body. They say that corporations have no soul, but they outlive men, and I have done what I think is best for the business and for everyone." Basta!

In the three decades following the Civil War, Pierce created an impressive, profitable, effective and architecturally cohesive group of buildings, a distinctly urban mill complex along the Neponset River. These Victorian commercial mill buildings, considered to be the finest extant mill complex in the city of Boston, are the highlights of the Lower Mills and Milton Village. The Lower Mills had, in the years following Pierce's lease of the Baker

Chocolate Company, gone from a small mill village to a distinctly urban industrial area. The mills had been built along both sides of Adams Street, where a company that had increased fortyfold under Pierce's ownership now employed hundreds of workers.

The noted Boston architectural firm of Bradlee, Winslow and Wetherell had carried out the design and building of the mill complex over three decades. With the use of red brick and similar architectural details, the architects successfully created a cohesive grouping of mills, each with a uniquely individual character. Following the death of Henry Lillie Pierce in 1896, the company was sold the following year to the Forbes Syndicate, which was headed by financier and Milton summer resident J. Murray Forbes. Forbes and other Boston investors purchased the ten thousand shares of the company for $4.75 million from the Henry Lillie Pierce Estate and continued to expand the physical plant that had begun in 1872. In the period between 1897 and 1927, the Forbes Syndicate built the Powder House (1906), the Ware Mill (1902), the Preston Mill (1903), the Forbes Mill (1911) and the impressive Baker Administration Building (1919). Not

A three horse–drawn delivery wagon stops in front of the Webb Mill on Adams Street in the early twentieth century. The wagon is packed high with wood boxes stenciled with the type of chocolate enclosed, awaiting transport to receivers. *Courtesy of Jane Schroth Lemire.*

An advertisement in the *Booklovers' Magazine* in 1905 had a woman pouring into a cocoa cup Baker's cocoa, which was said to be "pleasing to the taste, Nourishing to the system, Quieting to the nerves" and most importantly, "an Ideal food-drink—good morning, noon, and night."

A bird's-eye view of the Walter Baker Mills, circa 1920, by the Fairchild Aerial Surveys Inc. showed the area built up with mills on either side of the Neponset River. *Courtesy of Boston Athenaeum.*

only was the mill space doubled, but also the use of advertising in local and nationwide newspapers and magazines made Walter Baker & Company a household name.

The Forbes Syndicate began to invest heavily in lavish, full-page color advertisements in such nationwide magazines as *Liberty*, *Collier*, the *Youth's Companion*, the *Red Book Magazine* and the *St. Nicholas Magazine*. These beautifully illustrated advertisements touched on every aspect of American society, from the blond and blue-eyed child asking for a cup of Baker's Cocoa and young college men enjoying their cocoa as one of their sisters demurely pours at their fraternity house to World War I doughboys enjoying steaming cups of Baker's Cocoa rather than French wine in a small French inn. In one particularly engaging advertisement, Little Red Riding Hood approaches her grandmother's house with a basket full of chocolates and dainties, all made with real Baker's Chocolate. These colorful and artistic advertisements ensured that not only was Baker's Chocolate known and used by the general public but also its undisputed status as the oldest manufacturer of chocolate in the United States was reinforced by its skillful and adept marketing managers.

During this period, premiums were offered through the company for loyal customers, who could redeem coupons cut from cocoa tins and chocolate wrappers for bone china chocolate services with a cocoa pot, cups and saucers, all embossed with a profile of La Belle Chocolatiere. These sets were made in England by Shelley, in Germany by Dresden and in France by Limonges China Factories and were widely sought by the public. Other premiums included embossed serving trays, La Belle Chocolatiere bookends, silver-plated and sterling cocoa spoons and brooches bearing the image of the company trademark. However, the most sought-after giveaway was the annual cookbook that began as a small, twelve-page pamphlet in 1870 and eventually evolved into a lavishly illustrated, full color cookbook by the early years of the twentieth century. These cookbooks instructed one not only in the proper way to melt chocolate but also in how to prepare such elegant desserts as charlotte russe, chocolate éclairs and chocolate bombe, as well as old favorites such as chocolate cake, brownies and numerous types of fudge, including Wellesley, Vassar, Smith and Radcliffe fudge. In 1927, the Forbes Syndicate sold Walter Baker & Company to the Postum Cereal Company, now known as General Foods, which would continue the production of chocolate in the Dorchester Lower Mills and Milton Village until 1965, when the operation was moved to Dover, Delaware. In 1979, the company became a part of Kraft Family Foods.

Today, the Lower Mills offers an important example of a nineteenth-century mill village, incorporating commercial buildings within a diverse residential neighborhood. The mill village includes intact chocolate mills, with originally over fifteen acres of floor space and storehouses, as well as mill manager and millworker housing. Here, one can marvel at the mill complex that made chocolate and cocoa not only delicious products but also immensely profitable ones. The Baker Chocolate mill complex was primarily the work of Nathaniel Jeremiah Bradlee (1829–1888), Walter T. Winslow (1843–1909), George Homans Wetherell (1854–1930) and, after 1898, Henry Forbes Bigelow (1867–1929), well-known architects whose architectural partnership led to the design of numerous commercial, ecclesiastical and educational structures in Boston. The firm was known successively as Bradlee, Winslow & Wetherell; Winslow & Wetherell; and Winslow and Bigelow, but it was not until 1919, when Milton resident and noted architect George F. Shepard Jr. (1865–1955) of the Boston architectural firm of Shepard & Stearns designed the Baker Administration Building on the site of the former Hotel Milton, that the connection with the initial architectural firm came to an end.

HAIL QUETZALCOATL!
The God of the Morning Star

C hocolate! That creamy, rich, delicious confection we adore is something that few of us can resist, refuse or deny ourselves. Yet this sweet and decadent delicacy is something far different than what was enjoyed by our ancestors just a few centuries ago when it was a delicious and flavorful drink referred to as the "Food of the Gods."

The name *Quetzalcoatl* literally means "quetzal-bird snake" or "a serpent with feathers of the quetzal" in the Nahuatl language. The feathered serpent deity was important in art and religion in most of Mesoamerica for close to two thousand years, from the Pre-Classic era until the Spanish conquest of the sixteenth century. Civilizations worshiping the feathered serpent included the people of Central and South America—the Olmec, the Mixtec, the Toltec, the Aztec and the Maya. The worship of Quetzalcoatl sometimes included human sacrifices, although in other traditions that have come down to us, Quetzalcoatl was said to strongly oppose human sacrifice as a token of tribute. Mesoamerican priests and kings would sometimes take the name of a deity with which they were associated, so Quetzalcoatl and Kukulcan are also the names of historical persons. One noted Post-Classic Toltec ruler was named Quetzalcoatl, and he may actually be the same individual as the Kukulcan who invaded Yucatan at about the same time. In the tenth century, a ruler closely associated with Quetzalcoatl ruled the Toltecs, and his name was Topiltzin Ce Acatl Quetzalcoatl. This ruler was said to be the son of either the great Chichimeca warrior Mixcoatl and the Colhuacano woman Chimalman or one of their august and revered descendants.

The Toltecs were said to have had a dualistic belief system. Quetzalcoatl's opposite was Tezcatlipoca, who supposedly sent Quetzalcoatl into exile on a raft of snakes, with the promise to return. When the Aztecs adopted the

Montezuma and Cortes exchange gifts in a conjectural painting depicting the sharing of the coveted recipe for *chocolatle*, which was then brought to Spain, eventually sweetened for the western European palate and renamed cocoa.

culture of the Toltecs, they made twin gods of Tezcatlipoca and Quetzalcoatl, opposite in belief but equal in stature. Quetzalcoatl was also called White Tezcatlipoca, to contrast him with the Black Tezcatlipoca. Together, these twin, but different colored, gods were said to have created the world. The Aztec emperor Montezuma II initially believed that the landing of Hernando Cortes and the Spanish conquistadors in 1519 was in actuality Quetzalcoatl's long-awaited return, as was predicted when he left on the raft of snakes. Cortes played off this naïve belief to aid in his conquest of Mexico and the subjugation of the Emperor Montezuma II.

The exact significance and attributes of Quetzalcoatl varied somewhat between each of these civilizations and throughout history. Quetzalcoatl was often considered the god of the morning star, while his twin brother, Xolotl, was considered the evening star. As the morning star, Quetzalcoatl was known under the title Tlahuizcalpantecuhtli, which means literally "the lord of the star of the dawn." He was known and worshiped as the inventor of books and the lunar calendar, the giver of maize corn to mankind and sometimes as a symbol of death and resurrection. Quetzalcoatl was also the patron of the priests and held the revered title of the Aztec high priest.

Hail Quetzalcoatl!

Most Mesoamerican beliefs included the cycles of worlds. Usually, our current time was considered the fifth world, the previous four worlds having been destroyed by flood, fire and the like. Quetzalcoatl allegedly went to Mictlan, the somewhat mysterious underworld, and created the fifth world's mankind from the bones of the previous races (with the necessary help of Cihuacoatl), using his own blood to imbue the bones with new life. His birth, along with that of his twin, Xolotl, was unusual, as it was said to be a virgin birth, born to the goddess Coatlicue.

Quetzalcoatl was considered a god of such supreme importance and power that almost no aspect of everyday life seemed to go untouched by him. Secondly, as a historical figure, his actions would, and could, not be contained by history and thus eventually evolved into myth or revered legend. As a legend, he would signal the end of mortal kingship. An interesting phenomenon that distinguished Quetzalcoatl is that despite the fact that he is not considered to be the most powerful of gods within the Mesoamerican pantheon, or one of the eldest gods in the hierarchy, he is nonetheless an integral and vital part of the overall system. This was partially accomplished by his ability to integrate himself so securely to the attributes of his fellow brethren gods, to such an extent that it is virtually impossible to tell if Quetzalcoatl was the true originator. Hence, to assign a single definitive personality to a god is extremely difficult to do.

This lore was to become part of the Toltec, or Mexican, culture and has come down to us today as something far different than how it was perceived centuries ago. However, Quetzalcoatl is still revered as a god and one who obviously, like his mortal worshipers, enjoyed the savory drink *cacahuatl*.

Quetzalcoatl, also called White Tezcatlipoca, was the god of chocolate. The Aztec emperor Montezuma II initially believed that the landing of Hernando Cortes and the Spanish conquistadors in 1519 was in actuality the return of Quetzalcoatl, an event that was predicted when the god departed on a raft of snakes.

Chocolate as we know it today is the final, or end, result of a long process derived from the cultivation of the Theobroma cacao tree. This tree is a member of the malvales, an order of angiosperms that also includes the cotton plant. It grows in altitudes between 660 and 2,600 feet in warm, humid climates and in latitudes twenty degrees

The Theobroma cacao tree is a dwarflike tree that has cacao pods that grow from the branches, as well as the trunk, of the tree. These trees grow in warm climates and have been cultivated on plantations for centuries.

north and south of the equator, such as in Mexico, South America, the West Indies and the Caribbean, as well as the Gold Coast of Africa. It was enjoyed by the natives of these regions prior to its discovery by the Spanish explorers to the New World. Cacao trees are somewhat fragile, but those growing closest to the equator are said to be among the most fruitful, since temperatures below sixty degrees Fahrenheit may result in damage to the trees and thus to the next season's crop. The cultivation of tobacco and chocolate were two important luxuries that were to be exported to Western Europe by Cortes and the Spanish conquistadors.

The chocolate tree, known scientifically as the Theobroma cacao tree, thanks to eighteenth-century Swedish naturalist and father of taxonomy Carl von Linne (1707–1778), is a dwarflike evergreen tree growing an average of twelve to fifteen feet in height, with a silver-barked trunk from five to eight inches in diameter. When young, the Theobroma cacao tree is protected from the intensity of the sun by the planting of trees that give it shade; banana trees, lemon trees, coral trees and cotton trees are among those planted to shade the fragile Theobroma cacao trees. The protective trees are often referred to as the *madres del cacao* (mothers of the cacao), and they also help to protect the soil from drying out in the intense heat and sun.

The Theobroma cacao tree has branches spreading from its singular trunk, with large green leaves and small pink scentless flowers and numerous pods, which are grooved and irregular in shape and average from nine inches to a foot in length, growing from both the branches, as well as the trunk, of the tree. The oval-shaped cacao pods, when unripe and young, are green but

The flowers, fruit and seeds of the Theobroma cacao tree are depicted in this nineteenth-century print. There are upwards of twenty varieties of the cacao tree, each with its own distinct flavor that is imparted to chocolate.

20

The Theobroma cacao tree is said to usually mature within twelve years of planting and can continue to produce for upward of twenty-five years if nurtured.

The Theobroma cacao tree usually lives an average of thirty-five years, though the tree is pruned, shaded and cultivated annually.

Upward of 60 percent of the cacao pods simply dry up due to the intensity of the heat before maturity.

The cacao pods have forty to sixty beans, and the average weight of the useable beans per pod is five ounces.

The Theobroma cacao tree produces an average of two dozen cacao pods annually, with an average of three pounds of dried cacao beans from each tree.

A cacao plantation may not begin to see a profit until after six or seven years of cultivation.

Workers on a cacao plantation extract seeds from cacao pods and then spread them in thin layers on elevated boards to air and dry in the sun before they are placed in canvas sacks and shipped. *Courtesy of Andy Sawicky.*

slowly turn a dark yellowish brown as they ripen and are filled with beans or cacao seeds. These are encased in a membrane within the thick rind. The cacao seeds are the size of a thumbnail, and each pod has an average of forty to sixty seeds. The cacao pods are harvested when the ripe pods are cut from the tree by means of knives attached to long wood poles. The pods are then gathered in piles, where workers cut them open with a machete and scoop out the seeds and membrane. Oxidation occurs almost at once, causing the beans to turn brown. The beans are then spread on long low platforms in the direct sun so that they are only a few inches deep and will be allowed to dry. The beans ferment during the drying process, with the natural sugars swiftly turning to acetic acids. Once fully dried, a process that can take several days to a few weeks, depending on weather conditions, the cacao seeds are then manually cleaned of any pulp or membrane that remains and are bagged for shipment.

Although the Toltecs cultivated the Theobroma cacao tree for centuries, it was not until 1519 that the Spanish explorer and conquistador Hernando Cortes (1485–1547) learned of the secret of preparing *cacahuatl*, the delicious savory drink derived from the cacao seeds. Montezuma II, the emperor of

An eighteenth-century etching shows three men enjoying their drink of choice. On the left is an Arabian man enjoying coffee, in the center is a Chinese man enjoying tea and on the right is an Aztec man enjoying *chocolatle*, the savory chocolate drink.

the Aztecs, welcomed the Spanish at elaborate ceremonies where his guests were served this luscious, foamy drink in goblets. The honeylike drink was the crushed cacao seed, with the liquid being whisked to a froth and then flavored with vanilla and chili pepper and served cold. This was a refreshing but decidedly different drink from the sweet cocoa of the present day.

Cacahuatl was the Aztec name for the seeds of the tree from which this drink was produced, but the name was to become known as cacao to the Spaniards. The Indians of Mexico believed that the Theobroma cacao tree was of divine origin, and they highly valued the beans as not only a food but also a medium of exchange, as the beans were used as a form of currency. When Cortes returned to Spain, he was lauded for the introduction of the new drink, but the cacao beans were so highly prized that they were reputedly hidden in Spanish monasteries and remained a well-kept secret, only available to the wealthy since their price was

HOW TO MAKE CHOCOLATE, SIMPLIFIED

1. Cut the cacao pods from the Theobroma cacao tree. (There are more than twenty varieties of Theobroma cacao trees, and each variety has and imparts a different flavor to the chocolate. The trees can grow an average of fifteen to twenty feet in height, and the cacao pods grow from both the branches, as well as the trunk, of the cacao tree. Each cacao tree yields an average of 1 to 2 pounds of cacao beans, and an acre of cacao trees produces an average of 450 pounds of cacao beans.)
2. Split the cacao pods and scoop out the cacao beans, spreading them thinly and allowing them to ferment and to air and dry in the sun.
3. Bag and ship the cacao beans to the factory. (Once the cacao beans were received by Baker Chocolate, they were stored in silos until use, with no adverse effect whatsoever as they were dried. The silos built to the rear of the Park Mill had vertical holding containers that could hold many tons of dried cacao beans, with different types kept in separate storage silos.)
4. Clean and roast the cacao beans. (Once the cacao beans are removed from the silos, they are roasted. Once roasted, the cacao beans are cracked, the shells are removed and the nibs are put into storage.)
5. Blend the nibs for whatever chocolate is being made and grind them between granite stones to melt the cocoa butter, thereby forming a chocolate liquor that is the base of all chocolate products.
6. Pour the chocolate liquor into molds and allow it to solidify; the result is unsweetened baking chocolate.
7. Make cocoa by pressing the chocolate liquor to remove the cocoa butter, forming a cocoa cake. Once dried, the cocoa cake is ground into an exceedingly fine powder.
8. Combine chocolate liquor with milk, sugar, flavoring and other products to create chocolate such as milk chocolate, German sweet chocolate, Caracas sweet chocolate, Dot chocolate, etc.

prohibitive. Enjoyed in the sixteenth century by the Spanish royal family and the wealthy elite, chocolate was eventually introduced to France through the marriage of Anne, the daughter of Philip III of Spain, to King Louis XIII, who was a decided chocoholic. By the mid-seventeenth century, chocolate was being enjoyed outside the royal court of King Louis XIV and his queen, Maria Theresa.

The drink, once a refreshing savory drink flavored with vanilla and chili pepper, was sweetened with sugar and enjoyed as it is today as cocoa. In the eighteenth century, chocolate houses were opened and became fashionable resorts for patrons to enjoy a cup of cocoa. As demand increased, chocolate began to be produced throughout Europe. The concept of chocolate shops began in London, Florence and Vienna in the early eighteenth century, but it was in Vienna that a chocolate shop, in 1765, provided a backdrop for the fortunate meeting of an Austrian prince and a beautiful chocolate server.

CACAO ON THE NEPONSET

A River Where the *Latle of Chocolatle* Meant Water

The history of the Neponset River reaches far back in time, well past the settlement of Dorchester by the Puritans from the West Country in England in June 1630. The Neponset River was named by the Puritans after the Native Americans who first inhabited the lands, the Neponset tribe of the Massachusetts Indians. The Neponset Indians' chief, or sachem, was known as Chickatawbut.

The area that we refer to as the Lower Mills, which includes both Dorchester and Milton Village, is rich in recorded history. It was here, in 1633, that the Great and General Court of Massachusetts Bay Colony allowed Israel Stoughton to build a dam at the lower falls on the Neponset River to provide water power for his gristmill, on the express condition that he build a footbridge across the river. This gristmill, completed in 1634, was the first of its kind in New England and was to provide enough maize (ground corn) for the Puritans in the settlement, as well as for trade. The operation of the gristmill proved so efficient that there are records of the Pilgrims of Plymouth Bay Colony sending corn to be ground at Stoughton's Gristmill in Dorchester.

The Neponset River was forded by a bridge at the lower falls. It was not until 1662 that *Unquety*, or the town of Milton, was set off from the area we now know as Dorchester. The lands were rich and fertile, and corn, wheat and barley were grown in ample abundance. The ownership of the lands by the Puritans was to be strengthened in 1666, when Kitchamakin, sachem of the Massachusetts Indians, conveyed to the Town of Dorchester all the land "beyond the Neponsit [*sic*] Mill, to the utmost." By 1666, the Puritans had established complete and outright legal ownership of both the Neponset River and abutting lands, as well as the power generated by the

The Lower Mills and Milton Village, in an eglomise panel of 1808 showing the engine house of the Dorchester and Milton Fireward Society, the mills along the Neponset River and the arch erected over Adams Street in 1798. *Courtesy of Milton Historical Society.*

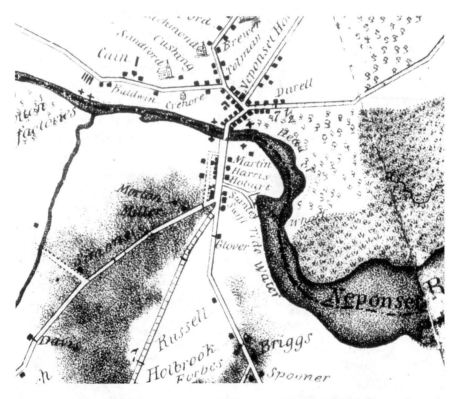

The Lower Mills and Milton Village flank the Neponset River. A detail of the map drawn in 1831 by Edmund James Baker shows the area of the chocolate mills, with residences and places of worship, all of which created a mill village.

river dam. Throughout the seventeenth century, growth continued, including the establishment of the first gunpowder mill and the first paper mill. The gunpowder, once dried, proved immensely important, as the Indian Wars commenced almost at once, and the new mill in Dorchester supplied the militias of Massachusetts Bay Colony with the necessary gunpowder to defend their settlements.

The Boies and McLean Mill produced, in 1728, the first paper pulp in America that was turned into sheet paper, a valuable and scarce commodity in colonial America. The mill, located on the south side of the Neponset River in Milton, was later managed by the Tileston & Hollingsworth Paper Company, whose Eagle Mill was opposite the Liveridge Institute on River Street. Then, in 1765, the fortuitous meeting of Dr. James Baker of Dorchester and John Hannon led to a joint venture in the production of chocolate. Cacao beans were roasted, ground and refined into what we know as chocolate in a rented mill on the Milton side of the Neponset River. The company was officially incorporated in 1780 as Baker's Chocolate and is accepted unequivocally as the oldest manufacturer of chocolate in the country. Three generations of the Baker family operated the mill from 1780 to 1852, but one of the most renowned owners of Baker's Chocolate was Henry Lillie Pierce, one-time mayor of Boston and for whom Pierce Square in Dorchester Lower Mills was named in 1895. Pierce was also stepnephew to Walter Baker.

John Hannon made chocolate from 1765 to 1779 that was wrapped in a paper label boldly embossed with "Hannon's Best" and the promise that "if the Chocolate does not prove good the Money will be returned." The scales of justice seem to back up this statement. *Courtesy of Milton Historical Society.*

Cacao on the Neponset

Throughout the nineteenth century, the Neponset River provided power for many diverse commercial interests. In addition to paper, chocolate and gunpowder, the first playing cards in the United States were produced by Crehore & Ford. The two partners, Benjamin Crehore (1765–1831) and Jabaz Ford, produced beautifully colored playing cards for many years, the forerunners of our playing cards of today. The first pianoforte was produced by Benjamin Crehore in Milton Village, in addition to the first bass viol and the first artificial leg ever seen in this land, made for Dean Weymouth, a veteran of the War of 1812. The cabinetmaking industry, located along the Neponset River, allowing case pieces to be shipped by water, was enhanced by Stephen Badlam, whose shop was at the corner of Washington and River Streets. Badlam was one of the finest cabinetmakers in America and produced furniture without rival. He lived and worked at the same time as Ebenezer H.R. Ruggles of Milton, who produced fine-quality Empire mahogany furniture, which is highly prized today.

One of the many attractions in the area was the Hotel Milton, which was a famous inn on the Dorchester side of the Neponset River, the present site of the Walter Baker Administration Building. It was opened in 1840 by Minot Thayer, a noted innkeeper who, in the early nineteenth century, had kept a tavern on Adams Street in Dorchester Lower Mills, now the site of Dunkin' Donuts. The Hotel Milton was known for many years as Thayer's Hotel and proved to be a popular stop with travelers either coming from or going to Boston along the King's Highway (present-day Adams Street).

Thayer's Hotel was a substantial, three-story, Greek Revival hotel, with a two-story front porch and Doric columns supporting an overhanging roof. It is said that in 1840 the first Roman Catholic Mass in either Dorchester or Milton for the large number of Catholic factory and granite industry workers was held at the hotel. Mass was, on occasion, continued there until 1863, when St. Gregory the Great Church was consecrated on Dorchester Avenue. By 1871, Thayer's Hotel was operated by William B. Brown, an employee of the Thayer family, who was quite an enterprising innkeeper. It was recorded in the *Saturday Evening Express* that his neighbors accused him of snaring pigeons, which led to the following locally popular ditty:

> *There was a hotel man named Brown,*
> *Whose house was the talk of the town,*
> *He found he was able*
> *To set a good table*
> *So long as the pigeons flew down!*

Thayer's Hotel did not share in the same comfortable carriage trade that patronized the Milton Hill House, but it still provided ample meals, libations and a comfortable overnight resting place for travelers.

Tallyhos were often rented by John Talbot from Henry Crane & Son's Lower Mills Stables on Derby Day in 1909 and frequently stopped in front of the Hotel Milton on Adams Street while being photographed by Frizzell, the village photographer. Mr. Talbot was proprietor of Talbot's Grocery Store, at 1157 Washington Street in the Lower Mills, which had traded since 1815 as much in alcohol as it did in groceries. He was also a real estate agent with offices at 85 Water Street in Boston. An avid horseman who later lived at 21 Canton Avenue in Milton Village, he often raced his trotting horses in the Dorchester Gentlemen's Driving Club and at the Readville Race Track in Hyde Park, which was laid out on the former Civil War Camp Meigs, named for Brigadier General Montgomery Cunningham Meigs (1816–1892), "soldier, engineer, architect, scientist, patriot."

The tallyhos, often amply filled with Mr. Talbot and eight of his friends, were pulled by "four-in-hands," which were often unmanageable by inexperienced drivers. On Thanksgiving Day 1908, Dorothy Forbes of Milton Hill recounted that Mr. Talbot's four-in-hand was

> *going down Milton Hill* [when] *one horse, much against the instinct of the other three, decided to run away. While still in the minority the Walter Baker factory whistle blew just as they went by, which started the other three horses at full speed. The fact that many of us on horseback, or in horse-drawn vehicles, chased the coach as best we could, kept this fair going the rounds of the town until the four-in-hand, both horses and those a-top the coach, were in a white lather.*

Walter Baker & Company, then owned by the Forbes Syndicate and headed by J. Murray Forbes (1845–1937), purchased the somewhat decrepit Hotel Milton in 1906 from A. Lizzie Mann, who had been renting it out to a variety of small businesses, including Cohen Brothers' Tailor Shop, Littlefield's Wallpapers & Steam Matting, W.F. Goward Dry Goods Store and Anton Gramer Furniture Store. There were also rented rooms above. The Forbes Syndicate demolished the building, and in 1919, the company commissioned Milton architect George F. Shepard Jr. (1865–1955), a partner of Frederick Baldwin Stearns in the premier Boston architectural firm of Shepard & Stearns, to erect its new brick and limestone office building. In 1920, upon its completion, they moved their business and mill offices from Boston to the new site.

The chocolate mill in 1765 was a small wood mill on the Neponset River that was operated by water power. Hannon and Baker used the mill for making chocolate and as a sawmill, as chocolate could not be made in summer months.

When we look at the Neponset River today, we see a swift current passing beneath our feet on the George Roper Bridge on Adams Street; however, few of us realize the vast importance our ancestors placed on the Neponset River and the power the river afforded numerous industrial concerns in the Lower Mills and Milton Village. The area was to see four competitors producing so much chocolate in the mid-nineteenth century that it was often referred to as Chocolate Village.

The first chocolate apprentice was Nathaniel Blake, who assisted John Hannon in the production of chocolate in the 1770s. However, it was the actual procuring of cacao beans that was a problem during the Revolution. The blockading of Boston Harbor by the British meant that cacao beans, and most other necessary goods, had to be smuggled into port. The laws that caused this and other problems came to be known as the Intolerable Acts. Hannon and Baker were able to continue production but probably on a reduced scale.

Beans were procured from various ports of origin and were cleaned and sorted at the mill. Next, they were roasted to bring out the particular flavor of each type of cacao bean. The roasting had to be maintained at a steady temperature and control, as under roasting left a raw taste, whereas over roasting created a highly pungent or even burnt taste. This process is probably the most important step and requires expert knowledge and skill—the ability to maintain success, but also the blend of the various cacao beans had to be the same each time to ensure the same flavor of chocolate.

The granite mill was a three-story mill on the edge of the Neponset River. By the time of the Civil War, the densely built-up area of the Dorchester Lower Mills, along Washington and Adams Streets and Dorchester Avenue, had evolved into the quintessential mill village. *Courtesy of Milton Historical Society.*

Once roasted, the cacao beans are milled, or slowly ground between large granite millstones powered by water power that are cut with a center hole and have grooved surfaces to allow rotation. The millstones were used well into the nineteenth century but were replaced with machinery that crushed the roasted cacao beans into such a refined powder that the liquid that is emitted is velvety smooth. Under heat and tremendous pressure, the cocoa butter from the mixture melts and combines with the beans to form glutinous chocolate liquor, which has a fragrant chocolate aroma. This chocolate liquor is then treated according to the type of chocolate that is to be made. For unsweetened chocolate (made by Baker's from 1765 to well into the 1840s), the chocolate liquor was simply poured into molds and allowed to set in cooling rooms. The result was a solid bar, or rectangular cake, of chocolate that could be scraped into boiling water for a delicious and refreshing drink.

Chocolate is a delicious confection if sweetened, but unsweetened chocolate made by Baker's Chocolate has a 53 percent cocoa butter content, which is an indication of its quality (the United States standard requires 50 percent). Baker's unsweetened chocolate is pure chocolate, with not an ounce of fat removed and nothing else added to it. For decades, this unsweetened chocolate was known and sold as Premium No. 1.

Cacao on the Neponset

In 1834, Walter Baker hired Mary and Christina Shields to work at the chocolate mill, a decisive step as the business was rapidly expanding. The Shields sisters were hired to wrap the bars of chocolate in paper, affix a printed label, box the wrapped bars and prepare them for shipment, but they were not the only women in the workforce. Baker also hired Martha Pond to work in what he referred to as the "secret room." This laboratory was said to be among the earliest in the food industry, and Baker's well-kept secrets in the production of chocolate were more than secure, as Miss Pond was a deaf-mute. According to the "Milton Anecdotes" of Eleanor Pope Martin, at

> *intervals, workmen headed for "the mill." Women in industry were the exception, but Walter Baker employed a few, among them Nancy Hunt and Hattie Baxter, who lived in a gambrel-roof cottage in "the Lane"* [now High Street in Milton Village]. *Attired in long, full skirts, and wrapped in large shawls, they decorously passed by, the epitome, it seemed, of proper and colorless maturity.*

With friendly competitors manufacturing chocolate on all sides, Baker was adamant about maintaining company secrets and his livelihood, as well as employing women in his chocolate mill.

Throughout the two decades prior to the Civil War, Walter Baker recognized the far-reaching and important advantages of advertising. He said in May 1842 to his agents, "I wish you would advertise our chocolate as often as once a fortnight at this season and in the Fall." He expressed concern that the quality of his chocolate remain consistently high and that agents return to him any chocolate products that were "worse for age, as the sale of it would be more injurious to me than its return." All of these procedures helped to ensure that only first-quality chocolate was available to the public and that the business could grow among competitive chocolate manufacturers.

In 1846, the Baker Mill was staffed with two workmen making chocolate, two apprentices learning the trade, six girls and a forelady. However, a disastrous fire in 1848 destroyed the mill. According to *A Calendar of Walter Baker & Company*, the granite walls were "so damaged by fire and water that it [was] necessary to take most of the building down."

In her wonderful narrative, "Milton Anecdotes," Eleanor Pope Martin comments on this fire and the commotion it caused. She made reference to a

> *spry, chipper, cherry little man who, bearing the name of Frederick William Karthouse Nye, and occupying the position of village druggist, dispensed*

A worker pauses at the corner of Adams Street and Baker Court as he sits on the buckboard of a horse-drawn watering cart that "watered" the streets and surrounding areas to the chocolate mills to cool the area during the warm summer months, as well as to keep down the road dust.

barley and checkerberry candy over the counter to an admiring horde. He was a great favorite among his friends, as well as with the children, the back room of his drug store being a favorite evening rendezvous. He never did things by halves. When the chocolate mill took fire one night, Mr. Nye, as a member of 90's Hose Company, without a moment's hesitation, rushed into the river with the hose, wading into mid-stream. The son of a New Bedford sea-captain, he naturally inherited a taste for drink, which was his one failing. "If you are going to <u>be</u> a fellow" he used to say to his intimates, "be a <u>hell</u> of a fellow!" The destroyed mill was promptly replaced by a new mill built of hammered granite that was designed by Gridley J. Fox Bryant (1816–1899), whose father had been involved in the Granite Railway Company. This new mill was considered a state of the art design but to preclude future problems Baker said "to prevent incendiaries making their way into the mill, I have had inside shutters [installed] *on all lower story windows.*

The 1850s were tumultuous years. Walter Baker died in 1852, and Sidney B. Williams died in 1854, stretching the company to its limits, but the leasing of the business to Henry L. Pierce in 1854 by the trustees of the Baker Estate proved a far-reaching and fortuitous decision for all parties involved. Over the next four decades, Pierce increased the company fortyfold and hired capable and honest men to manage his business while he served as mayor of Boston and as United States congressman and when he traveled abroad to inspect chocolate-making concerns in England, France, Switzerland and Germany. By 1868, there were forty-eight employees, twenty-three of whom were women, and Pierce began the expansion of the mills with the building of the Pierce Mill, which was designed by Nathaniel J. Bradlee, in 1872. The expansion of the physical plant between 1872 and 1919 was tremendous, but it was the consistent high quality of the chocolate and cocoa that enabled the business to see such tremendous growth.

Baron Justus von Liebig (1803–1873), noted German chemist who made significant contributions to the analysis of organic compounds and the application of chemistry to biology and agriculture, was quoted in the 1893 edition of Baker Chocolate's *Choice Recipes*, stating that chocolate

> *is a perfect food, as wholesome as delicious, a beneficent restorer of exhausted power; but its quality must be good, and it must be carefully prepared. It is highly nourishing and easily digested, and is fitted to repair wasted strength, preserve health, and prolong life. It agrees with dry temperaments and convalescents; with mothers who nurse their children; with those whose occupations oblige them to undergo severe mental strains; with public speakers, and with all those who give to work a portion of the time needed for sleep. It soothes both stomach and brain, and for this reason, as well as for others, it is the best friend of those engaged in literary pursuits.*

In 1886, it was said in *Cocoa and Chocolate*:

> *Frequent analyses have been made, under the direction of Board of Health and sanitary associations in our large cities, to determine the purity of chocolate and cocoa preparations sold in this country, and in every such analysis the articles manufactured by Walter Baker & Co., are reported to be entirely pure and free from the admixture of deleterious substances.*

Among the various types of chocolate and cocoa made by Walter Baker & Company, Ltd., were:

> *Baker's Premium No. 1 Chocolate: The pure product of carefully selected cocoa beans, to which nothing has been added and from which nothing has been taken away. Unequalled for smoothness, delicacy and natural*

**WALTER BAKER & CO'S
PREMIUM No. 1 CHOCOLATE**

FAC-SIMILE OF ½ LB. PACKAGE.

A bar of Baker's Premium No. 1 was wrapped in blue paper, with a cream-colored label that said the chocolate was a "nutritive, salutary, and delicious beverage, for more than a century!"

In an 1846 advertisement of Walter Baker & Company's broma, the opinions of eminent physicians of Boston were solicited and unanimously stated that "from knowledge of its ingredients, we think it will be useful to invalids and persons recovering from disease…It also offers good nourishment for Children." *Courtesy of Andy Sawicky.*

flavor. Sold in a blue paper wrapper (later a cardboard carton) with a yellow label.

Cocoa: A perfectly pure and refreshing beverage, prepared exclusively from selected cocoa. It is safely recommended to those who wish a wholesome preparation, combining all the properties of the cacao beans.

Baker's Vanilla Chocolate: Guaranteed to consist solely of choice cocoa and sugar, flavored with pure vanilla beans. It is the best sweet chocolate in the market and [is] used at receptions and evening parties in place of tea and coffee.

Caracas Chocolate: A delicious chocolate, good to eat and to drink. It is one of the finest and most popular sweet chocolates on the market and has a constantly increasing sale in all parts of the country.

Century Chocolate: A fine vanilla chocolate for eating and drinking.

German's Sweet Chocolate: One of the most popular sweet chocolates sold anywhere; it is palatable, nutritious and healthful, and a great favorite with children.

Dot Chocolate: A high-grade, slightly sweetened chocolate specially prepared for homemade candies and for sportsmen's use.

Auto-Sweet Chocolate: A fine eating chocolate, enclosed in an attractive wrapper with an embossed representation of an automobile in various colors.

Broma: A preparation of pure cocoa and other highly nutritious substances, pleasantly flavored and sweetened. It contains a large proportion of theobromine and possesses powerful restorative *qualities. Its delicacy of flavor and perfect solubility* [have] *made it a favorite drink among thousands. Medical men of all shades of opinion recommend it to their patients instead of tea or coffee.*

Cocoa Nibs: Freshly roasted beans cracked into small pieces. The nibs contain no admixture and present the full flavor of the cocoa bean in all its fragrance and purity. When properly prepared, it is one of the most economical drinks.

Falcon Cocoa: A preparation for the special use of druggists and others making hot or cold soda. It forms the basis for a delicious, refreshing, nourishing and strengthening drink.

Caracas and Vanilla Tablets: Small pieces of chocolate, made from the finest beans and done up in fancy foil. These tablets are put up in small cartons and packages tied with colored ribbons, and are very attractive in form and delicious substance.

Breakfast Cocoa: By a peculiar process in the manufacture of this article, the theobromine and nutritive portions of the cocoa are preserved with more than double the strength [than] *other preparations contain, and the delicious natural flavor of the nut is fully developed. For persons with delicate constitutions and weak nerves, it is unrivalled as an article of diet, and it is equally beneficial in maintaining the physical and mental vigor of those who are in health. It adds strength to the body, new life to the exhausted brain, quiets the nervous system, harmonizes the workings of the digestive organs and gives purity to the blood. The Breakfast Cocoa being a comparatively new preparation, some grocers may not yet have added it to their stock.*

Racahout des Arabes: A most nutritious substance, [it] *has become indispensable as an article of diet for children, convalescents, ladies and delicate or aged persons. It is composed of the best nutritive and restoring substances, suitable for the most delicate system. It is now a favorite breakfast beverage for ladies and young persons, to whom*

A trade card for Racahout des Arabes extolled the virtues of this agreeably flavored cocoa that was said to be "free from the exciting qualities of coffee and tea" and "a favorite breakfast beverage for ladies and young persons, to whom it gives freshness and embonpoint."

A BRIEF TIMELINE OF THE
BAKER CHOCOLATE COMPANY

1765   *Dr. James Baker financially backs John Hannon, an enterprising Irish immigrant with the skill of making chocolate, in a rented mill on the Milton side of the Neponset River. Hannon labels his chocolate "Hannon's Best Chocolate" from 1765 to 1779.*

1779   *John Hannon reputedly sails to the West Indies to purchase cacao beans but disappears. It is rumored that he fled his wife, Elizabeth Gore Hannon, and returned to Ireland.*

1780   *Dr. James Baker acquires Hannon's share from his "widow" and establishes the Baker Chocolate Company, labeling each of his chocolate bars "Baker."*

1791   *Edmund Baker, son of Dr. James Baker, enters into partnership with his father.*

1804   *Dr. James Baker retires from the company, and Edmund Baker assumes ownership.*

1818   *Walter Baker, son of Edmund Baker, enters into partnership with his father.*

1824   *Edmund Baker retires from the company, and Walter Baker assumes ownership.*

1852   *Walter Baker dies, and Sidney Williams, brother-in-law of Baker, assumes ownership.*

1854   *Sidney Williams dies, and Henry Lillie Pierce, step-nephew of Walter Baker, assumes control, leasing the business.*

1884   *Henry L. Pierce is finally allowed to purchase the company from the trustees of the Baker Estate.*

1895   *The company is incorporated as the Walter Baker Company, Ltd.*

1897   *The company is purchased by the Forbes Syndicate.*

1927   *The company is purchased by Postum Company, Inc., a division of General Foods, and the name is changed to the Walter Baker & Company, Inc.*

1966   *General Foods moves the operation to Dover, Delaware.*

1989   *Kraft Foods acquires General Foods and the Baker Chocolate name.*

it gives freshness and embonpoint. It has solved the problem of medicine by imparting something that is easily digestible and at the same time free from the exciting qualities of coffee and tea, thus making it especially desirable for nervous persons or those afflicted with weak stomachs.

Racahout des Arabes has a very agreeable flavor, is easily prepared and has received the commendation of eminent physicians as being the best article known for convalescents and all persons desiring a light, digestible, nourishing and strengthening food. [This preparation was later known as Cacao Des Azteques.]

THE FRIENDLY COMPETITORS

The people who make constant use of chocolate are the ones who enjoy the most steady health, and are the least subject to a multitude of little ailments which destroy the comfort of life.

B aker's Chocolate is today one of the best-known, and most importantly the oldest, chocolate manufacturers in the United States and is known to most shoppers by its distinctive trademark logo of La Belle Chocolatiere on every chocolate bar or bag of chocolate chips, but it was not the only manufacturer of chocolate in the area of the Lower Mills in the nineteenth century. In 1768, Edward Preston, the future brother-in-law of Dr. James Baker, installed chocolate-making equipment in the rented mill of Barlow Trecothic at the Dorchester Lower Mills. Daniel Vose operated a small mill that produced chocolate, as well as paper, and a prosperous coastwise trading company. Thus, the sweet competition began, with four individual companies eventually manufacturing chocolate in the area prior to the Civil War.

PRESTON'S CHOCOLATE COMPANY

Edward Preston (1744–1819) married Lucy Bowman, the daughter of Reverend Jonathan Bowman of the Dorchester Meeting House in 1764, and would eventually become the brother-in-law of Dr. James Baker when Baker married his wife's sister, Lydia Bowman. Preston was to install chocolate-making equipment in the rented mill of Barlow Trecothic in 1768, which had previously been used as a woolen fulling mill. Preston must have carried on the business alone for the next few years, but in 1773 he signed a receipt stating that he received from James Baker "one Pound Thirteen shillings &

Four Pence in full, for my part of the Rent of the Chocolate Mill, until the 11th of Dec. 1772." In 1775, Preston's barn and chocolate mill in Dorchester were destroyed by fire, causing John Hannon, who was making chocolate in the mill, to relocate to the Boies Mill, where he took Nathaniel Blake as an apprentice to learn the process of making chocolate. However in 1780, the year after John Hannon disappeared on a reputed trip to the West Indies, Preston was hired by Dr. James Baker to manufacture his chocolate, as Preston had rebuilt his fulling mill and also fitted up a chocolate mill. This caused business to increase rapidly, but in 1788, Preston discontinued making chocolate for his brother-in-law.

By 1812, Preston had taken his son John into his chocolate business. A gristmill to grind maize was added that year to the cloth and chocolate manufactory. Upon the death of the founder in 1819, John Preston continued the business, which, by 1835, was said to be making an average of 750 pounds of chocolate per day. The Preston Chocolate Mill continued as a "friendly competitor" of the other chocolate manufacturers, but in 1859, John A. Preston and Walter Preston, great-grandsons of Edward Preston, sold the chocolate mill and business to Henry D. Chapin, who then sold it to Henry Lillie Pierce a year later.

WARE CHOCOLATE COMPANY

Dr. Jonathan Ware (1797–1877) was a chocolate manufacturer in Milton Village, and his company was known as the Ware Chocolate Company. A graduate of Brown University in 1821, he had previously served as an assistant to Dr. James Mann, surgeon in the hospital in Burlington, Vermont, during the War of 1812. Dr. Ware came to Milton in 1828, and three years later he was married to Mary Ann Tileston (1804–1884), sister of Edmund Pitt Tileston, a manufacturer of paper with Amor Hollingsworth in the firm of Tileston & Hollingsworth at a mill at the Upper Falls, or what is today Mattapan, Massachusetts. In *The History of Milton, Massachusetts 1640–1887*, Ware was said to have had

> *for many years a large* [medical] *practice in Milton and adjoining towns. He enjoyed the confidence and respect of his patients, and his name is spoken of, by those of them who still live, with affection. In his medical views he was holistically liberal, trusting largely to nature rather than to drugs. Decided in his opinions, he was ready to learn of others. With good common-sense and medical tact. A kind friend and an honest man.*

It was said that Dr. Ware gained local notoriety for his often repeated comment, "Well! If people would only rest, there wouldn't be occasion to take so much medicine!" In 1840, Dr. Jonathan Ware built a mill adjacent to his home at Milton Village where he set up two grinding wheels, one for grist and one for chocolate, and became the third competitor, after Baker and Preston, to produce chocolate along the Neponset River.

His headstone in the Milton Cemetery states that he was "for fifty years a physician in Milton," and he strongly extolled the virtues of chocolate as a healthy food choice. He was one of six eminent physicians of Boston who stated their opinions in the 1876 edition of *Choice Recipes*, published by Walter Baker & Company:

> *We have tried the BROMA manufactured by Mr. Walter Baker, of Dorchester, and find it a pleasant article of food. From knowledge of its ingredients we think it will be useful to invalids and to persons recovering from disease, especially to such as dislike the articles usually recommended. It also offers good nourishment for Children.*

In addition to Ware, this group of eminent and well-respected physicians included Drs. John Collins Warren, George Hayward, John Homans, Walter Channing and Zabdeil Boylston Adams.

Chocolate obviously was not just delicious but was also promoted by physicians as actually being good for you!

WEBB & TWOMBLEY CHOCOLATE COMPANY
(later known as the Webb Chocolate Company)

Another one of the "friendly competitors" was the Webb & Twombley Chocolate Company, founded in 1843 by Josiah Webb (1811–1888), a native of Skowhegan, Maine, and Josiah F. Twombley (1815–1875). Opening their chocolate mill in a rented mill owned by Dr. Jonathan Ware, another chocolate manufacturer on the Milton side of the Neponset River and a local physician, they produced a fine-quality product that would ensure that their business continued for nearly four decades.

The Ware Mill, built in 1839 on the site of the old mill erected in 1708 by Joseph Belcher, was located on the north corner of Adams and Eliot Streets in Milton Village, which was also the site of the first paper mill in New England, founded in 1728 by Daniel Henchman, Gillum Phillips, Benjamin Faneuil, Thomas Hancock and Henry Deering. This is the present site of the Webb

The Webb Mill, designed by Bradlee & Winslow and built in 1882, is at the corner of Adams and Eliot Streets in Milton Village. On the right are the Baker Mill and the Hotel Milton, later the site of the Administration Building.

Mill, which was built in 1882 and designed by the noted Boston architectural firm of Bradlee & Winslow, an architectural partnership of Nathaniel J. Bradlee and Walter Winslow, for Henry L. Pierce, then president of the Baker Chocolate Company. Josiah Webb had previously been a coal dealer in Dorchester, and Josiah Twombley was a teamster, with a route between Dorchester and Boston, prior to their partnership; however, beginning in 1843, with a chocolate maker hired from the Preston Chocolate Company, they began the production of Webb & Twombley's chocolate and cocoa.

Obviously, in addition to Baker's Chocolate and Dr. Ware's Chocolate, Webb & Twombley was to further contribute to the delicious and heady aroma of chocolate in the Lower Mills, or Chocolate Village. With swift success, it became a competitor of Walter Baker, who, in May 1843, wrote a deeply concerned letter to John P. Mott, his former secretary and the brother of his late wife, about the competitors' new chocolate business. Baker said that Josiah Webb and Josiah Twombley had

> *been making cocoa paste, which Mr. Child is said to have pronounced as*
> *good as mine. Now, Twombley could never learn this art of making paste*
> *in this country but from me, Freeman or yourself, as none others know it*

and as I have not taught him...I hope you have truth enough in you to state without reservation or equivocation what lessons you have given him to injure your benefactor.

This "sharing of the secrets" in the chocolate business directly affected Baker's business, but it obviously wasn't something new, as it had occurred almost a century earlier between Dr. James Baker and his soon to be brother-in-law, Edward Preston. Dr. James Baker had, in 1765, financially backed the Irish-born chocolate maker John Hannon in a rented mill in Milton Village, producing the first chocolate in colonial America. Three years later, Edward Preston (who was married to Lucy Bowman, sister of Dr. Baker's future wife, Lydia Bowman Baker) installed chocolate-making equipment in Barlow Treothic's mill in Dorchester and began the production of chocolate. The friendly competition in the production of chocolate was evident, but by 1780, Dr. Baker had become the sole owner of the mill, after Hannon's disappearance at sea in 1779, and he began to produce chocolate in earnest, marking each bar of chocolate "Baker."

In 1850, Webb & Twombley's increased business over the previous seven years allowed it to move to a new mill. Operations were moved from the Dorchester side of the Neponset River to Milton Village at Adams and Eliot Streets, the present site of the Webb Mill. This partnership continued successfully until 1861, when Twombley sold his share of the business to Webb, and the enterprise was henceforth known as Webb's Chocolate Company. Josiah Webb continued in the manufacture of chocolate and cocoa for two more decades, until July 1, 1881, when he sold his business to Henry Lillie Pierce, president of Baker's Chocolate Company. Interestingly, Pierce had

Webb's Chocolate was established in 1843 and was originally known as the Webb & Twombley Chocolate Company. This circa 1865 trade card shows a young woman enjoying a cup of cocoa. In 1881, Josiah Webb sold his business to Henry L. Pierce.

a new mill built on the site of the former competitor's mill at Adams and Eliot Streets in Milton Village. He named it the Webb Mill, in recognition of his former competitor in the chocolate business.

In an etching from 1887, the Webb Mill stands as an impressive five-story red brick and rough-hewn brownstone Romanesque Revival mill in Milton Village, with pedestrian, carriage and wagon traffic crossing the bridge spanning the Neponset River. On Morton Hill can be seen the original Milton Hill House, then operated by Theodore Train Whitney as a comfortable resort. On the lower right is Talbot's Grocery Store, which later moved to the Bispham Block designed by Joseph Tilden Greene and built on the rise of Washington Street between Adams Street and Miller's Lane in the Lower Mills (now resident parking for the Baker Chocolate apartments). Today, the Webb Mill is the site of Milton Hill Sport & Spa, a health club overlooking Milton Village and the Neponset River. Gym-toned patrons exercise where chocolate manufacturers and workers once produced a product with a heavenly aroma that brought about the moniker Chocolate Village.

HENRY LILLIE PIERCE

The Man Who Created a
Victorian Chocolate Empire

In 1896, the City of Boston named the intersection of Dorchester Avenue and Washington and Adams Streets in Dorchester Lower Mills "Pierce Square" in memory of Henry Lillie Pierce. Today, few residents of the area know that this is the official name of the Lower Mills intersection, nor are they familiar with the myriad accomplishments of the man for whom it was named.

Henry Lillie Pierce (1825–1896) was the son of Colonel Jesse Pierce (1788–1856) and Elizabeth Vose Lillie Pierce (1786–1871) of Stoughton, Massachusetts. His father had been an educator at Milton Academy and later served in the Massachusetts House of Representatives. As a gentleman farmer, he maintained a large farm in Stoughton (formerly a part of Dorchester) until he moved, in 1849, to Washington Street in the Lower Mills of Dorchester with his wife and two sons. Edward Lillie Pierce was then attending Brown University, while Henry Lillie Pierce was at Milton Academy and was to later attend the Bridgewater Normal School.

In 1849, Henry L. Pierce was hired to work as a clerk at the Baker Chocolate Company. Walter Baker, the owner of the chocolate company and stepbrother of Pierce's mother, hired him at a salary of three dollars per week. However, as their political views invariably clashed and caused tremendous animosity (Pierce was a vociferous and deeply opinioned Free-Soiler), Pierce left after only a year of politically tinged employment to take up newspaper work in the Midwest. At the request of Sydney Williams, brother-in-law of Baker and managing director of the chocolate mill, Pierce returned to Boston after a year and was appointed manager of the Walter Baker Counting House at 32 South Market Street in Boston (now a part of the Quincy Market retail area). Pierce was obviously a hard worker, for after the deaths of both Walter Baker (in 1852) and Sydney Williams (in 1854), he was permitted to lease the chocolate

Henry Lillie Pierce

Henry Lillie Pierce (1825–1896) was president of Walter Baker & Company from 1854 until his death. His portrait was painted in Paris, in 1895, by Joseph F.L. Bonnat and shows a confident and successful businessman who had increased his business fortyfold in four decades. *Courtesy Museum of Fine Arts, Boston, 2009.*

business from the trustees of the Baker Estate.

The trustees of the Baker Estate, fully aware that Pierce had only been with the company for five years, leased the business to him for a two-year probationary period, "subject to a life interest payable annually to Mrs. Baker," widow of the late owner and stepaunt to Pierce, until her death in 1891. He began manufacturing under the name and style of Walter Baker & Company. He was obviously successful, for in 1856 the trustees extended the lease a further eight years, during which time Pierce began an expansion that would eventually absorb his competitive chocolate manufacturers in the Lower Mills. The trustees continued the ten-year lease until 1884, when "all terms under the Walter Baker will having been satisfied, the entire property is conveyed by the Trustees to Henry L. Pierce." In 1860, Pierce bought the Preston Chocolate Mill from Henry D. Chapin, to whom it had been sold the previous year, and in 1881, Josiah Webb sold his chocolate mill to Pierce.

In 1864, the trustees of the Baker Estate renewed the lease for a second decade. This decade was decisive for Pierce, as he began to enter his chocolate in competitive exhibitions both in this country and abroad. In 1867, Baker's Chocolate and Cocoa won an award in the Paris Exhibition for the quality of the product. In 1873, the company won the highest awards at the Vienna Exhibition, and in 1876, at the Philadelphia Centennial, Walter Baker chocolate and cocoa won the highest awards. With mill managers and mill employees, Pierce was able to expand the chocolate business and build new mills. In 1894, these were equipped with chocolate-making machines, most of which were imported from Germany, that saved power and were easy to attend.

Pierce followed in his father's footsteps and was elected to the Massachusetts House of Representatives from 1860 to 1862, and again in 1866; he also served in the Forty-third and Forty-fourth Congresses from 1873 to 1877. His interest in not only his employees but also the voters of Dorchester made him a very popular choice. After Dorchester was annexed to the city of Boston on January 4, 1870, Pierce was nominated and elected mayor of Boston in 1872 and 1877. It was during his terms as mayor that Pierce's business began an extensive marketing and public relations campaign to make Walter Baker & Company a household name or, better, the household choice for chocolate and cocoa. In 1883, the company formally adopted the trademark La Belle Chocolatiere as its logo. Used earlier in the company's history, this famous design was copied from the pastel portrait of *Das Schokoladenmadchen* by Jean-Etienne Liotard, an eighteenth-century Swiss painter. The chocolate girl was to become as famous as the company she promoted. It was not until 1884 that the trustees of the Baker Estate allowed Pierce to purchase the company outright. Once done, it was incorporated as Walter Baker & Company, Ltd.

Pierce was honored by the City of Boston when the school committee voted in 1892 to name the new grammar school just south of Codman Square in his honor. The school was designed by Boston city architect Harrison H. Atwood (1863–1954) and was an enormous hammered granite building at the corner of Washington Street and Welles Avenue (now the site of the Codman Square Branch of the Boston Public Library). It was considered one of the most advanced schools in the Boston public school system, and after the Great Depression, its focus became that of a "Baking School," which offered trade classes.

During Pierce's ownership of Baker Chocolate Company, from 1854 to 1896, he was to increase business greatly, so much so that he created an urban mill village with modern chocolate mills along the Neponset River. His budget for advertising and marketing was tremendous, but none was more important than the adoption of La Belle Chocolatiere as his trademark. He employed women to dress as the trademark come to life in silk gowns, with crisply starched white lawn aprons, caps and cuffs. They would act as demonstrators at exhibitions and fairs, where they offered samples of Baker's Chocolate to those in attendance. These demonstrators, with comely faces and ready smiles, were an important and appropriate way to advertise his product. An article in the *New York Times* on October 21, 1892, reports that these demonstrators were at an exhibition at the Madison Square Garden in New York City, where it was said that the "taste of the chocolate is its own sufficient advertisement, but the combination of chocolate and girl is particularly effective." The article went on to say that at this food show,

*one of the most noticeable exhibits of this sort is made by Walter Baker &
Co., who occupy a conspicuous place just opposite the main entrance to the
amphitheatre. Under a silken canopy, disposed as was the canopy at old
Ashby, wherein Lady Rowena watched the conquering arms of the young
King Ivanhoe, a cluster of pleasing damsels dispenses the soothing "tap"
of Baker. All are dressed in the costume of "La Belle Chocolatiere" of
Liotard's painting in the Dresden Gallery, made familiar to everybody as
the trademark of this old established firm. The soft draperies of the canopy
are a pleasing frame for the quaint costumes and brilliant complexions of
the chocolate girls, and even rival exhibitors praise the taste shown by the
firm in displaying its wares so attractively.*

These comely demonstrators, who elicited the praise of even the rival
exhibitors at an exhibition, were only one aspect of Henry Lillie Pierce's
astute ability to attract attention to his products.

In her book *Crowding Memories*, Mrs. Thomas Bailey Aldrich, widow of
the former editor of the *Atlantic Monthly*, wrote of Pierce as a close friend to
her and her husband. She said that for "nearly twenty-five years…[he had]
been one of the most loved of guests at our fireside." Pierce's "deep and
unaffected friendship" for the Aldriches was sincere, and they, like many
others, benefited from his estate, inheriting his farm at Ponkapoag in Canton,
Massachusetts. Mrs. Aldrich summed up his character, saying that he was

*in all ways a strong man. Strong in will even to obstinacy, strong in his
sense of honor, strong in his love for his friends, strong in his sympathies,
strong in his patriotism, strong in his likes and dislikes. To those who knew
him best there was a certain charming simplicity in his character due to
the fact that it was the clear and direct product of his nature, unhelped by
outside influences.*

Upon his death, Henry Lillie Pierce remembered each and every one of his
employees with a gift of $100. His public bequests included one to Harvard
that, at the time, was the largest such gift the college had ever received. Pierce
also left equal sums to the Museum of Fine Arts, the Massachusetts Institute
of Technology, the Massachusetts General Hospital and the Homeopathic
Hospital, and it was said that "not in a long time has there been known
such generous remembrances of public institutions and charities as in the
provisions of his will."

THE MIGHTY EXPOSITIONS
AND EPHEMERA

Expositions are the timekeepers of progress.
—*William McKinley*

EXPOSITIONS

In the mid-nineteenth century, the Crystal Palace Exposition in London, England, highlighted the vast achievements of industry and commerce, and hundreds of exhibitors gathered to offer their examples under glass-topped buildings. The great cast-iron and glass palace was designed by noted architect Joseph Paxton and built in the London suburb of Hyde Park, where it extolled the tremendous success of the Industrial Revolution with a mind-boggling fourteen thousand exhibits from all parts of the world, including India and the countries with recent European settlements, such as Australia and New Zealand, constituting the new far-flung empire of Queen Victoria. Many of the visitors who flocked to London to see the exposition came from all parts of Europe and the United States. The Crystal Palace, which was in part the brainchild of Prince Albert, consort to Queen Victoria, was widely acclaimed for its important and far-reaching venue, and its tremendous success would be emulated by other expositions throughout the world in the following decades.

Henry Lillie Pierce, after he assumed control of the Baker Chocolate Company in 1854, began an expansion plan not only of the physical plant, through the planned building of new mills, but also of the chocolate and cocoa themselves, through widespread marketing. As early as 1867, Pierce had boldly entered Baker chocolate and cocoa in the Paris, France exhibition, where it was awarded a prize for its quality. In fact, in the *Paris L'Indicateur* it was said that *alluding to the silver medal* [the highest] *awarded to this house at the Paris Exposition of 1867, the Paris "L'Indicateur" says "France, until the present time, has always held the first rank in the production of this article* [chocolate], *but it seems generally admitted by the most competent judges that this year Walter Baker & Co., of Boston, have taken precedence over all other manufacturers in this line of goods."*

In 1873, Baker chocolate and cocoa were to win the highest awards at the Vienna Exposition, and in 1876, they won the highest awards at the Philadelphia Centennial. These exhibitions, both abroad and in this country, were tremendously important, as millions of visitors came to savor samples of chocolate and cocoa and thereby learn of the high-quality chocolate product produced by Pierce in Dorchester Lower Mills. Among the exhibitions in the United States that Walter Baker & Company entered and where it received medals and diplomas were the Maryland Institute (1852, 1853); Mechanics' Institute, Boston (1853, 1878); Franklin Institute, Philadelphia (1853); American Institute, New York (1853); Crystal Palace Institute (1853); Mechanics' Institute, Cincinnati (1855); Paris Exposition (1867, 1878); Mechanics' Institute, New Orleans (1871); Vienna Exposition (1873); United States Centennial Exposition (1876); Mechanics' Institute, San Francisco (1877); Southern Exposition, Louisville (1883); and the World's Industrial Exposition, New Orleans (1884). So prominent and respected had this venerable company become that, according to *Choice Recipes*, in 1876, the centennial of the United States, it was said that "amid all the changes which have taken place, amid the wars and rumors of wars, and the financial panics, this house has stood firm, doing an honest and legitimate business, and maintaining its credit and integrity unimpaired."

In 1901, at the opening of the Pan-American Exposition in Buffalo, New York, United States president William McKinley gave an address, and in his speech he included the following poignant and thought-provoking words:

Expositions are the timekeepers of progress. They record the world's advancements. They stimulate the energy, enterprise, and intellect of the people, and quicken human genius. They go into the home. They broaden and brighten the daily life of the people. They open mighty storehouses of information to the student.

Among the many expositions that made a decisive impact on the cocoa and chocolate business through increased sales, due in part to the huge amount of positive publicity, were:

1876 Philadelphia Exposition
Philadelphia, Pennsylvania

The Centennial International Exhibition was the first official exposition in the United States and was held in 1876 to celebrate the 100th anniversary of the signing of the Declaration of Independence in Philadelphia. It was officially known as the International Exhibition of Arts, Manufactures and Products of the Soil and Mine. It was held in Fairmount Park, located along the Schuylkill River. The fairgrounds were designed by noted architect Hermann J. Schwarzmann (1846–1891). The Main Building of the Philadelphia Exhibition was designed by well-known architects Henry Pettit (1842–1921) and Joseph M. Wilson (1838–1902) and was constructed of cast iron and brick. It had an enormous display floor of twenty acres that was dedicated to the exhibits of both foreign and domestic manufactured goods.

This exposition was truly the gala celebration of the United States' centennial. At the same time, the exposition was designed to show to the

The Baker Chocolate Pavilions at the expositions were architect-designed and often fanciful and interesting structures, only intended to last a few months. The Pan-American Exposition's pavilion had a tile roof, with parapets bearing the trademark, as did the fancifully decorated entrance.

world the United States' vast industrial and innovative prowess since the advent of the Industrial Revolution. The centennial was originally set to begin in April 1876 to suitably commemorate the anniversary of the Battles of Lexington and Concord, but inevitable construction delays caused the date to be pushed back to May 10, 1876. When the exposition did open, albeit late, bells were rung all over Philadelphia. The festive opening ceremony was attended by United States president Ulysses Simpson Grant and his wife, Julia Dent Grant, as well as Brazilian emperor His Majesty Dom Pedro.

The creation of an exhibit of a "colonial kitchen," replete with an open fireplace for cooking, a beehive oven, a spinning wheel and costumed presenters, sparked an era of "Colonial Revival" in American architecture and house furnishings. Among the unique displays showcased at the exposition were the right arm and the torch of the Statue of Liberty, sculpted by Frederic Auguste Bartholdi (1834–1904) and commissioned by the Union Franco-Américaine. Bartholdi purportedly modeled the face of the statue on that of his mother and the body after his mistress. For fifty cents, visitors could climb the ladder to the balcony surrounding the flame of the torch, and the money raised was used to fund the rest of the statue, which was eventually, in 1886, to be donated to the United States.

1893 World's Columbian Exhibition
Chicago, Illinois

The World's Columbian Exposition was held in Chicago from May 1 to October 31, 1893, to celebrate the 400th anniversary of Christopher Columbus's discovery of the New World. The fair had a profound effect on late nineteenth-century architecture, the arts and Chicago's self-image, as well as American industrial optimism. The Chicago Columbian Exposition was, in large part, designed by well-known architect and urban planner Daniel Hudson Burnham (1846–1912) following the principles of Beaux-Arts design, namely, the principles of European Classical architecture, which were based on design symmetry and balance.

The exposition covered more than six hundred acres, with almost two hundred new buildings of European architecture and people and cultures from around the world. Over 27 million people (about half the U.S. population) attended the exposition over the six months it was open. Its scale and grandeur far exceeded the other exhibitions of the time and became symbols of the tremendous industrial growth of America since the Civil War.

The exposition was located in Jackson Park and on the Midway Plaisance in the neighborhoods of South Shore, Jackson Park Highlands, Hyde Park and Woodlawn. The layout of the fairgrounds—which included a Wooded Island, lagoons and canals, as well as ponds and basins—was created by renowned landscape architect and acknowledged "Father of American Landscape Architecture" Frederick Law Olmsted (1822–1903), and the grounds were embellished with impressive white stucco buildings designed by such prominent architectural firms as McKim, Mead and White; Peabody & Stearns; Carrere and Hastings; Richard Morris Hunt; Van Brunt & Howe; George B. Post; and Louis Sullivan.

The Baker Chocolate pavilion was designed by the prominent New York architectural firm of Carrere & Hastings, a partnership of John M. Carrere and Thomas Hastings. It was said to have cost $60,000 for an impressive pavilion only intended to be used for six months. The two-story white stucco building had flanking staircases that ascended to large windows that opened from a balcony to a large reception room. The pavilion was located between the Manufacturers Hall and the Music Hall, opposite the monumental Statue of the Republic, which was created by noted American sculptor Daniel Chester French (1850–1931.)

Margaret S. MacGillivary, former secretary of Henry Lillie Pierce, said:

> *It is hard for anyone not close to the scene to realize the tremendous growth of the business in a short span following the World's Fair in Chicago, which proved a tremendous advertisement for Walter Baker & Company.*

1894 California Midwinter International Exposition San Francisco, California

The California Midwinter International Exposition, commonly referred to as the Midwinter Exposition or the Midwinter Fair, was a world's fair that operated for six months in San Francisco's sixty-acre Golden Gate Park. Its most enduring legacies are the M.H. de Young Memorial Museum and the park's famed Japanese Tea Garden. The exposition was the brainchild of Michael H. de Young, then editor and sole proprietor of the *San Francisco Chronicle*, and James Phelan, a successful San Francisco businessman. In 1892, United States president Benjamin Harrison had appointed Phelan a national commissioner to the World's Columbian Exposition, which was held in Chicago, Illinois, the following year.

In 1894, Walter Baker & Company erected this fanciful Moorish-inspired pavilion at the Midwinter International Exposition in California. Demonstrators await visitors at the multi-arched entrance with an Arabian dome proclaiming "Cocoa" above.

1901 Pan-American Exhibition
Buffalo, New York

The Pan-American Exhibition was organized by the Pan-American Exposition Company, formed in 1897. Cayuga Island was initially chosen as the place to hold the exposition because of the island's proximity to Niagara Falls, which was a huge tourist attraction and would thereby attract a wide spectrum of society.

After the war, there was a heated rivalry between Buffalo and Niagara Falls over the location. Buffalo won out for two main reasons. First, Buffalo had a much larger population; with roughly 350,000 people, it was the eighth-largest city in the United States. Second, Buffalo had better rail connections; the city was within a day's journey by railroad for over 40 million people. In July 1898, the United States Congress pledged $500,000 for the exposition to be held at Buffalo.

Another helpful factor was that a three-phase system of alternating current power transmission for distant transfer of electricity had recently been invented. It allowed designers to light the exposition in Buffalo using power generated twenty-five miles away at Niagara Falls.

The exposition is most remembered today because United States president William McKinley was unfortunately shot by anarchist Leon Czolgosz on September 1, 1901, and died within days of his wounds.

1904 St. Louis World's Fair
St. Louis, Missouri

The attention of America and the entire world turned to St. Louis and the 1904 St. Louis World's Fair. St. Louis hosted "The Greatest of Expositions" for seven months, attracting visitors from near and far. David Rowland Francis was the driving force behind the fair, serving as president. He had also served as mayor of St. Louis, governor of Missouri and United States secretary of the interior and would later serve as United States ambassador to Russia. By far the largest of the several Victorian-era world's fairs, it occupied over twelve hundred acres at the western edge of St. Louis, including the western half of Forest Park. Also referred to as the Louisiana Purchase Exposition, the fair commemorated the centennial of the 1803 purchase of territory from France that more than doubled the size of the United States. Though originally planned to take place in 1903, the fair was delayed by one year in order to complete the construction of state and foreign buildings and to permit the gathering of the thousands of exhibits. One of the major reasons the fair was so successful was that the 1904 Olympic Games, the third in modern history and the first in the United States, were held in St. Louis during the fair.

From April to December 1904, the St. Louis World's Fair displayed the art, science and cultures of the entire world. Over twelve million visitors paid fifty cents' admission to marvel at the exhibits and magnificent buildings. Numerous foreign countries and hundreds of manufacturers and companies gathered in St. Louis to offer an unsurpassed display of civilization, history and culture. On display were the latest manufacturing products and processes, scientific inventions and innovations, agricultural advances and famous paintings, sculptures and art treasures.

Among the many manufacturers was the Walter Baker & Company, whose exhibit was a two-story, Colonial-style building with arched doors and windows and projecting balconies on the second floor. The first floor had a large exhibition room with an exhibit of chocolate and cocoa and how they were made. There were glass jars filled with cacao pods, cacao beans, shells, cracked cocoa and cocoa butter on display, as well as the end product of

A group of demonstrators create a *tableau vivant*, replete with cocoa cups, in 1900. These demonstrators were an important feature in the marketing of Baker's cocoa and chocolate, and the women went to church fairs, agricultural fairs and world expositions with ready smiles and engaging personalities.

cocoa and chocolate. Cocoa was available for visitors, and chocolate samples were handed out by demonstrators dressed as La Belle Chocolatiere. One of the major attractions was a working model of the chocolate machine made in Germany especially for this exhibition. It was operated by its own motor and showed the process of making chocolate from the cacao beans that arrived from various ports.

A lecture room was also located on the first floor, and here, at regular intervals, Miss Burr of the Boston School of Domestic Science, a regular contributor to the annual cookbooks and recipe books published by Baker Chocolate, lectured on scientific cookery with chocolate.

On the second floor was a large serving room, with a small kitchen operated by Baker Chocolate employees, where Baker's vanilla chocolate and cocoa were served to visitors. The rooms were filled with antiques, as well as large tin portraits of La Belle Chocolatiere, framed lithographs of the mills in Dorchester and Milton, Massachusetts, and exhibits that were marvels to both children and adults alike.

1907 Jamestown Exhibition
Jamestown, Virginia

The Jamestown Exposition was planned to celebrate the 300th anniversary of the 1607 founding of Jamestown, Virginia, the first successful English colony in the New World. In 1901, at the instigation of the Association for the Preservation of Virginia Antiquities and the Tidewater Commercial League, the General Assembly of Virginia authorized the governor to proclaim the tercentennial of the landing at Jamestown to be celebrated in 1907. The General Assembly granted a charter to the Jamestown Exhibition Company to hold the exposition. Governor Fitzhugh Lee was elected president of the company. Due to the efforts of the citizens of Norfolk, the Tidewater area was chosen for the approximately 340-acre exposition site.

Walter Baker & Co.'s Cocoa and Chocolate preparations have held the market with constantly increasing sales for 129 years and have received 52 highest awards in Europe and America.

A writer on dietetics says: "The use of a thoroughly reliable preparation of cocoa should be universally encouraged, and it is the consensus of opinion among medical men as well as laboratory workers that the breakfast cocoa manufactured by Walter Baker & Co. Ltd., not only meets the indications, but accomplishes even more than is claimed for it."

A new and handsomely illustrated recipe book sent free to any address

WALTER BAKER & CO. Ltd.
Established 1780   DORCHESTER, MASS.

Edwin J. Lewis Jr. designed a "New England Cottage—Period of 1780" for the Jamestown, Virginia Exposition of 1907. Here, demonstrators greeted visitors in a house of the period during which Dr. James Baker had established his chocolate mill. They offered cocoa and other delicacies made from a "new and handsomely illustrated recipe book," which was sent free to any person requesting one.

The project was not completed by the opening day on April 26, 1907, and the planned Historic Art and Education Buildings remained incomplete by the exposition's end in late November. President Theodore Roosevelt had opened the exposition with great éclat and presided over the naval review. After the impressive ceremonies on opening day, attendance dropped sharply and never again achieved projected numbers.

As originally laid out, the Jamestown Exposition grounds included twenty-one state buildings arranged in two equal rows separated by five blocks of grounds, with both rows facing north over Hampton Roads. Located between the two groups and set back three blocks were the History Building and the Auditorium, with its two detached wings. Walter Baker Co., Ltd., commissioned noted Boston architect Edwin J. Lewis Jr. (1859–

Walter Baker (1792–1852) was the grandson of the founder of the chocolate mill. Educated at Harvard College, and later studying law with Judge Tappan Reeves, he was a successful businessman who steadily increased the business while legally protecting it from competitors.

1937) to design a New England cottage of the period of 1780, the year the company was established by Dr. James Baker, as its home at the exhibition. This two-story, wood-framed, center-entranced house had a center chimney and a welcoming pair of parlors on either side of the front hall, where demonstrators welcomed guests.

Of the surviving state buildings, only the Georgia, Maryland, Missouri, North Dakota, Ohio, Pennsylvania, Virginia and West Virginia structures remain on their original sites. The Delaware building is an example of a colonial homestead with a gable roof and dormers. The Georgia building was modeled after the home of President Theodore Roosevelt's mother, Georgia native Marta Bulloch. The Maryland building is a replica of Homewood in Baltimore. The North Dakota building is a bungalow-style cottage. The Virginia and West Virginia buildings are Georgian Revival in style, and the Pennsylvania building is a replica of Independence Hall, Philadelphia. The Baker Chocolate cottage was reputedly moved to Milton, Massachusetts, where it was sold as a residence.

The nineteen remaining buildings of the 1907 Jamestown Exposition form a rare surviving collection of Edwardian exposition buildings and were listed in the National Register of Historic Places on October 20, 1975.

These were only a few of the many exhibitions into which Henry Lillie Pierce, and later the Forbes Syndicate, entered the chocolate and cocoa of Walter Baker & Company from 1854 to 1927. However, it was also the ephemera of the company that became an important advertising and marketing tool.

EPHEMERA

The Walter Baker Chocolate Company was founded by Dr. James Baker in 1780 and is considered the oldest manufacturer of chocolate in the United States, as well as one of the earliest companies to offer a money-back guarantee on the quality of its product. In many ways, the founding of the first chocolate mill in the United States would prove important to the well-being of the American public. A 1905 advertisement of Baker's Chocolate quoted Jean Athleme Brillant-Savarin as saying, "Those who make the constant use of chocolate are the ones who enjoy the most steady health, and are the least subject to a multitude of little ailments which destroy the comfort of life." He was certainly qualified to justify chocolate consumption; Brillant-Savarin (1755–1826) was a politician, magistrate, gastronome and author of *The Physiology of Taste*. From its beginnings in a rented mill on the banks of the Neponset River in Massachusetts, the Baker Chocolate Company eventually grew into one of the largest industrial concerns in the area, as well as the largest chocolate manufacturer in the United States in the nineteenth century.

From a fortuitous meeting between Dr. James Baker and John Hannon, the business continued to grow through three generations of the Baker family: Dr. James Baker, his son Edmund Baker (1770–1846) and his grandson Walter Baker (1792–1852).

After the death of Walter Baker in 1852, the trustees of his estate leased the company to Henry L. Pierce (1825–1896), stepnephew to Baker, for three decades before he was allowed to purchase the business. He increased the business fortyfold over the ensuing four decades. Between 1880 and 1920, the rapid expansion of the business and the astute marketing plan of Baker's Chocolate led to some of the most interesting and colorful trade cards and ephemera to be produced in the United States during this period. The instantly recognizable La Belle Chocolatiere soon became synonymous with the company. With a wide array of broadsides, trade cards, calendars, cookbooks and related collectibles, the Walter Baker Chocolate Company became well known not just locally but also internationally. In many instances, the company's demonstrators (modern-day versions of La Belle Chocolatiere) went to exhibitions, church fairs, agricultural shows and even prominent European expositions in Paris, London and Vienna, where their skillful mastering of Baker's Chocolate (learned through the easy-to-follow directions in *Choice Recipes*), engaging personalities and ready smiles made the public's first impression of the company a pleasant one.

An advertisement of Walter Baker & Company, circa 1850, shows a maiden with a cornucopia full of chocolate, chocolate paste, cocoa and broma. The Baker office was on South Market Street in Boston's Quincy Market, and the delicious product was "for sale by all the principal grocers in the United States."

Shortly after Henry Lillie Pierce's death in 1896, the Baker Chocolate Company was purchased by the Forbes Syndicate, which was headed by financier J. Murray Forbes. Forbes immediately began to advertise the chocolate and cocoa in nationwide magazines that included *Country Life in America*, the *Nicolas Magazine*, the *Youth's Companion, Collier's* and *Harper's Weekly*. Usually full page and in color, these images were to become ingrained in the public's mind through a constant stream of artistic ads that purported that Baker's Chocolate and Cocoa were loved by not only children, fraternity men, theatre actresses and World War I doughboys in France but also the ever popular Little Red Riding Hood, who no longer approached Grandmother's house with anything less than a basket of Baker's Chocolate and Cocoa. In so doing, the Forbes Syndicate made Baker's Chocolate synonymous with the general public and reiterated that it was "known and loved" by generations of Americans—something its competitors could not possibly lay claim to.

During this artistically productive period, the calendar was published in 1900. This six-page calendar, printed by the Barta Press of Boston, dealt with six generations (considering twenty years per generation) that had known and loved Baker's Chocolate since its founding. The 1840 image was of a young woman reclining on a sofa with a bearded doctor seated beside her, administering chocolate by the spoonful. The caption reads, "Doctors now recommend Baker's Chocolate as a 'beneficent restorer of exhausted power. A perfect food, preserves health, prolongs life, soothes both stomach and brain.'" The 1900 image had the quintessential Gibson Girl posing

1900

WALTER BAKER & CO. LTD.

now lead the world in the manufacture of COCOA & CHOCOLATE

This is the last of a series of 7 advertisements accurately representing the fashions at stated periods between 1780 and 1900. The set will be sent free to any applicant. Address

WALTER BAKER & CO. LIMITED, BOSTON, MASS.

In 1900, Walter Baker & Company advertised "the fashions at stated periods between 1780 and 1900" and how each generation of Americans had known and loved Baker's cocoa and chocolate. The quintessential "Gibson Girl," in her elaborate gown and upswept hair, stands in her foyer enjoying a cup of Baker's cocoa.

in a form-fitting gown with a cup of Baker's Cocoa in her hand. If this sixth-generation descendant of La Belle Chocolatiere, seen in a pendant on the right of the 1900 image, continues to drink her delicious cocoa, let's hope she is able to keep her hourglass figure in the process! Other advertisements included an art nouveau treatment of a mother and daughter who enjoy their Baker's Cocoa out of cups and saucers, into which the cocoa is poured from a Baker's Chocolate cocoa pot. Colorful, engaging and instantly eye-catching, this advertisement boasts that Baker's is "the Finest Cocoa in the World" and has received "40 highest awards in Europe and America."

In many ways, these advertisements were the most important marketing tool, barring the actual tasting of the chocolate, because they could appeal to residents of Boston as well as those of San Francisco. These nationwide magazines were an important feature in disseminating information, especially as it was done in such an attractive and interesting way. However, one aspect of this marketing tool was to prove more important than anything else: *Choice Recipes*, the lavish cookbook printed annually that was both handsomely illustrated and sent free to those asking for a copy. Beginning in 1870, these recipe books began as small, unillustrated booklets that instructed one on how to properly melt chocolate and combine it with other ingredients to produce such mouth-watering items as fudge, candies, cakes and brownies. By the turn of the twentieth century, these cookbooks averaged sixty pages or more and not only included recipes for Vassar, Smith, Wellesley and Radcliffe fudge but also those for chocolate éclairs, chocolate jelly, chocolate oysterettes and chocolate charlotte. By carefully following the tried and true recipes, you too could make confections and sweets to impress your family and friends. Beautifully illustrated and often in full color, these cookbooks had a short introduction to the nutritional value of chocolate by nutritionist Ellen Swallow Richards. Mrs. Richards graduated from Vassar and was the first female graduate of the Massachusetts Institute of Technology; she later founded the New England Kitchen in Boston's South End, which provided inexpensive but highly nutritious foods to the large immigrant population of that neighborhood. Her articles, which extolled the virtues of the nutritional value of chocolate and regularly appeared in Baker's *Choice Recipes*, can often lessen our guilt over the indulgence of chocolate!

Today, Baker Chocolate advertisements, broadsides and cookbooks (*Choice Recipes*), as well as the eagerly sought-after premiums, such as pencil sharpeners, trays, cups and saucers, cocoa pots, La Belle bookends, ashtrays, La Belle tin tables and a plethora of other items, are hot collectibles, but when we think of the company's founding on the banks of the Neponset River, we remember it as a "Delicious Memory from the Past."

THE FORBES SYNDICATE AND POSTUM-GENERAL FOODS

It was a great place to work.
—Donald Blair

In 1895, Henry Lillie Pierce incorporated the company as Walter Baker & Company, Ltd. and was recorded as having said to his ever faithful secretary, Margaret S. MacGillivary, "The die is cast. Walter Baker & Company is now a corporate body. They say that corporations have no soul, but they outlive men, and I have done what I think is best for the business and for everyone." However, the death of Henry Lillie Pierce the next year was to prove a great loss, as well as a harbinger of decisive change in the operation of the chocolate mills.

Pierce died at the Beacon Hill home of his friend Thomas Bailey Aldrich (1836–1907), poet, novelist and editor of the *Atlantic Monthly*, where he was spending the evening prior to his departure on a trip to Europe. In forty-two years, Pierce had increased Baker & Company fortyfold and thereby amassed an immense fortune, much of which he left to charity. However, he did not forget that his four hundred employees were a large and very important part of his success. The eighteenth clause of his lengthy will read:

> *To each person, male or female, who shall be in my employment or service as an operative, laborer, or domestic (including all hands at the mill) at the time of my decease, except those who are herein specifically named as legatees, I give $100.00.*

The business was purchased in 1897 by a syndicate composed largely of Boston capitalists, including J. Murray Forbes, and referred to as the Forbes Syndicate. The cost was $475 a share for the ten thousand shares of the concern, for a total of $4,750,000.

Henry Lillie Pierce was not just president of Walter Baker & Company from 1854 to 1896, but he also served as mayor of Boston in 1872 and 1877 and as a United States congressman.

Within a short period of time, according to *A Calendar of Walter Baker & Company*, the new syndicate was "having the largest trade in history of the Walter Baker chocolate business, and will have to make an addition in our machinery during the coming year."

In the next two decades, the company instituted benefits that would directly help the workforce, which had increased steadily. In 1904, all employees with one year or more service received a week's salary as extra compensation. The company also reduced the workweek from fifty-eight hours to fifty-six hours; the ten-hour day was from 7:00 a.m. to 11:45 a.m. and from 1:00 p.m. to 5:45 p.m. In recognition of the Adamson Act, in 1916, the company adopted an eight-hour day as the basis, with time and a half for extra hours up to a maximum of sixteen hours. Employees were also offered a cooperative group life insurance plan.

In this exciting period, Hugh Clifford Gallagher served as president of Walter Baker & Company, Ltd. He had initially been employed by Josiah Webb at Webb Chocolate Company and came with the acquisition of that chocolate competitor when Henry Pierce purchased the business in 1881. He was respected by Pierce and often traveled with him to expositions, as well as, in 1894, to Europe to purchase chocolate-making machines that were more efficient and more easily operated. During the period from 1895 to 1927, there was a dramatic increase in the importing of cacao beans, with 24 million pounds of cacao beans in 1893 and an incredible 275 million pounds by 1921. This increased demand for chocolate was partly due to the widespread enjoyment of cocoa and chocolate snack bars in the United States, as well as the fifty-five different types of chocolate produced. Baker's Chocolate saw dramatic increases in production and profit.

It was the consistent quality of its product that ensured Baker & Company's sustained success. Guarantee sheets stating the high quality and purity of the chocolate and cocoa reassured the public of the company's commitment to quality. Gallagher continued to expand the business and to order new machinery, especially from Bothfeld & Weygant of New York. He traveled to expositions, as had Pierce, and his visit to the Paris Exposition in 1900 confirmed the well-respected and favorable light in which the general public held Baker's Chocolate. He recorded in his diary during his stay in Paris that the "display of chocolate confectionery, in comparison with the Exposition of '89, would lead me to think that there has been a great growth in that branch of the business during the past ten years."

Gallagher continued Pierce's vision and expanded the mill complex, building the Ware Mill in 1902 and the Preston Mill in 1903. Both mills were designed by the Boston architectural firm of Winslow & Bigelow, successor firm of Nathaniel Bradlee, who had begun the rebuilding in 1872 when he designed the Pierce Mill. The mills were named for two former chocolate competitors, the Ware Chocolate Company and the Preston Chocolate Company, and with the building of the Power House in 1906 and a refrigeration plant in 1907, the physical plant had been doubled in size. The Power House was a decisive improvement with a high impact on production, as it contained three boilers, two large generators, electric lights and motors in the mills, and most importantly, it allowed for an expansion of the time in which chocolate could be produced. Previously, horse-drawn sprinkler tanks had watered lawns and walkways surrounding the mills during the heat of the day in an effort to cool the surrounding air of the mills.

In the early twentieth century, the once important use of horses in the business began to decline. Horses had been stabled on the mill complex for decades, as they provided the horsepower necessary to move chocolate and cocoa. There were ten single-horse teams to carry supplies from storehouses to various mills; two four-horse teams that went to Boston daily with cocoa and chocolate for stores, ships and trains; and a four-horse show team that was impressive, as well as a well-used marketing tool. By 1913, several electric-powered trucks had been purchased, and the horses were gently phased out of the business.

John Gordon was employed to oversee the horses and stables from 1903 to 1924, and during this time the original twenty-nine horses were reduced to ten in 1920, as electric- and gasoline-powered trucks were doing the work. In 1909, the first electric-powered truck was purchased, two more trucks arrived in 1911 and another was bought in 1912. In 1913, another electric truck was purchased and was to be operated by James Fitzsimmons for the

WALTER BAKER & CO'S MILLS-DORCHESTER,MASS.

1. A bird's-eye view of the mills of Walter Baker & Company in 1900 showed, from the left, the Adams Mill, the Pierce Mill, the Preston Mill, the Webb Mill and the Baker Mill.

2. A Baker's breakfast cocoa tin tray was produced in 1907 to commemorate the Jamestown, Virginia Exposition, complete with the Edwin J. Lewis Jr.–designed *New England Homestead* in the lower center.

3. Preston Chocolate Company was founded in 1768 by John Preston, brother-in-law of Dr. James Baker. This advertisement has vignettes with the Boston office and Dorchester mill, families at table, boxes and bags of cacao beans and shells and transportation, all in an elaborate scroll design. *Courtesy of Boston Athenaeum.*

4. The Chicago Exposition of 1893 was a major marketing coup for Walter Baker & Company. The New York firm of Carrere and Hastings designed the two-story white marble exhibition building, replete with twin staircases, balconies and a large hall where demonstrators greeted visitors.

Above: 5. Various products of Walter Baker & Company were advertised in this elaborate broadside, including American and vanilla chocolates, prepared cocoa and broma, as well as homoeopathic cocoa. An eagle and American flags surmount a cartouche flanked by an Arabian and American frontiersman, with the mills, wharf and train distribution points below.

Left: 6. Artist Norman Price depicted Little Red Riding Hood approaching Grandmother's House in this 1916 advertisement, with "a basket of Christmas dainties with Baker's Cocoa and Chocolate" on her arm and a large spray of holly to surprise her grandmother, hopefully before the wolf arrives!

7. A circa 1855 lavishly illustrated broadside of Walter Baker & Company advertised its various products, including chocolate, cocoa, broma and cocoa paste, in addition to homeopathic and dietetic cocoa. The tropical scene with cacao plants and pods is enhanced by a woman holding a cacao pod on the lower right. *Courtesy of Boston Athenaeum.*

Above: 8. A circa 1873 advertisement of the Pierce Mill showed Walter Baker & Company's medals in the four corner vignettes, the "highest premiums awarded a the principal exhibitions of the world." *Courtesy of Boston Athenaeum.*

Left: 9. Chocolate cake, held aloft by Mother as her son returns home from school and the family dog stares in delight, was said to be "so nice when made with real Baker's Chocolate." Confidently called the "finest of cooking chocolates," Baker's was identifiable by its blue wrapper and yellow label.

10. By the mid-1940s, Walter Baker & Company had expanded its manufacture of breakfast cocoa, Premium No. 1 chocolate, Dot sweet chocolate and German's sweet chocolate to include Post's Bran chocolate, Baker's milk chocolate bars and Baker's sweet chocolate tablets, which were circular disks of sweet chocolate covered in a candy.

Left: 11. During World War I, it was said in this advertisement that "somewhere the boys are drinking a Baker's cocoa toast to mothers, fathers, wives or sweethearts," with the poignant statement that the chocolate is as "delicious as dreams of home."

Below: 12. Eagle Chocolate was a superfine product "à la canelle" made by Walter Baker & Company in the Eagle Mill in Dorchester. *Courtesy of Earl Taylor*.

Horse-drawn wagons were loaded with boxes of wrapped chocolates and cocoa tins at the storehouses before delivering the products to shipping points in Boston. The wagons were covered with tarps to protect the easily damaged chocolate from the warmth of the sun.

conveying of chocolate to and from the different mills. In 1914, a Walker Electric truck was purchased, and the company continued to implement more efficient timesaving services.

WORLD WAR I

The United States declared war against Germany and entered World War I on April 16, 1917. Employees enlisted to serve in the war and were promptly replaced by a higher percentage of female employees and retirees. The operation saw the production of a chocolate bar that was stamped with the initials "WTW," or "Win the War," which was provided as part of the soldiers' kits. Chocolate maker Joseph D. Beal remembered:

> *After the boys left to join the army forces at the front in France, we could not get much sugar to use. What chocolate we did make was eating chocolate for the soldiers, and only one kind of coating chocolate, in ten pound cakes.*

In an attractive advertisement during this period, doughboys, or World War I Allied soldiers, are seated at a table in a French inn, being served cocoa

The Walter Baker Administration Building, designed by George F. Shepard Jr. and built in 1919, commanded the streetscape in 1970. Flanked on the left by the Forbes Mill and on the right by the Pierce Mill, the bridge spanning the Neponset River had become a major connector from Boston to the South Shore communities. *Courtesy of Ann and George Thompson.*

by a woman who looks remarkably like La Belle Chocolatiere. It was an important part of the production during the war, but the chocolate marked "WTW" brought great renown and widespread awareness to the company as hundreds of thousands of veterans returned to the United States and sought the same chocolate they had enjoyed during the war.

The expansion in 1919 of the mill complex with the building of the Administration Building had a major impact on the streetscape, with the Classical Revival design by George F. Shepard Jr. differing from the earlier mills. The continued expansion for the first two decades of the twentieth century led to the need for a larger workforce, which in turn meant increased benefits to retain employees and, in 1924, a hospital for medical treatment with a full-time trained nurse on duty at all times of operation and a doctor who had regular office hours. This period of growth was a decisive one and was, in many ways, perceived by managers and employees as a combined effort of all.

In 1926, William B. Thurber became president of Walter Baker & Company, Ltd., following on the great strides and expansion of the business made by Hugh Clifford Gallagher. A year after his election, ownership of the chocolate company was transferred to Postum Company, Inc. On August

12, 1927, Walter Baker & Company, Ltd., officially became known as the Baker Division of General Foods, and the following employee benefits were continued, and in most cases expanded, under its administration:

Cooperative retirement plan
Vacation with pay for all regular employees
Sickness benefit plan
Termination allowance plan
Group life insurance plan

Federal Labor Union No. 21243 of Dorchester Lower Mills, affiliated with the American Federation of Labor, was also established.

Following the acquisition of the chocolate company by General Foods, the line of confectionary chocolate was greatly expanded. The first milk chocolate was produced in 1928. Competitors in the United States, such as Hershey's and Mars, had been making confectionary chocolate for years, and General Foods was well aware that it needed to compete for a foothold in this market. In the next decade, the expansion of this confectionary line was to see "readily edible" chocolate that could compete with other manufacturers of chocolate candy not just in the United States but also in Europe. Baker's new confectionary line included semisweet chocolate bars, almond bars, milk chocolate bars, mint wafers, rum and butter wafers and milk chocolate bars in mocha, coconut and cashew varieties. This new confection line was so well received that a Cincinnati newspaper stated in April 1930, "General Foods Wins Record Sales with $1,000,000 More Advertising." It went on to say that the

> *Walter Baker bars are enabling General Foods to enter the confectionary field and drug store outlets for the first time. Retailing at five and ten cents, they have been tested for several months in New England and New York State.*

With the aid of the 1929 Hawley-Smoot tariff laws, which aimed at eliminating foreign competition in order to stabilize the competitors, General Foods expanded not only the Baker Chocolate Division but also its many other food-related companies. In 1941, General Foods had twenty-eight companies in its food production empire, which was to dramatically increase to over fifty companies by 1950. General Foods had ensured its place as a major food production and distribution company in the United States, and the Baker Chocolate Division had proven itself to be not just a delicious

Demonstrators stand beneath a larger-than-life portrait of Anna Baltauf at the top of the stairs in the Administration Building. Each woman holds a tray of cocoa cups or plates of chocolate delicacies made from one of the *Choice Recipe* cookbooks distributed by the company annually.

venue but also a valuable and major asset to General Foods. The company continued its long-standing practice of strict quality control, instituted under both Pierce and Gallagher, which ensured the consistent production of quality-made chocolate and cocoa. According to *A Calendar of Walter Baker & Company*, a scientific laboratory was maintained and staffed for "the sole purpose of marking each batch of Baker products to prepare for quick identification in the event of an injury" or any questions on production. By the early 1940s, the company had expanded its offerings to the public by adding "recipe-friendly" items that were delicious and also saved valuable time and expense for a more cost-conscious public. Among these new time-saving offerings was an instant cocoa mix that could be used to make either hot or cold cocoa in an instant, as well as chocolate fudge, cake frosting and chocolate sauce. This offering was taken up with alacrity by housewives across the country and was a great success from the start.

The Forbes Syndicate and Postum-General Foods

In 1941, General Foods decided to build eighteen storage silos and a grain elevator adjacent to the Park Mill Building, as it was said in the 1941 *General Foods Annual Report* that "our previous storage facilities were needed by the Government." There were nine pairs of monumental concrete silos attached to a long concrete core that was used to store dried cacao beans. According to Donald Blair, an employee of General Foods at the Baker Chocolate Division for many years, the cacao beans

> *came in burlap bags from all over the world and were dumped into a conveyor belt and then someone had to direct which individual silo it went into by bean type. The floor was flat and covered the entire area, but each silo had a hatch on top so you could get into it; this was necessary from time to time as the beans would get stuck together and hang up. When that happened, and when they tried everything else to dislodge them, they would lower a guy down through the hatch in a bosun chair, and he would chop away at the stuck beans until they came loose. They gave everybody that worked in the production/shop area uniforms, and they also laundered them so you always had clean ones, as some jobs were quite messy and dirty.*

The silos were eighteen circular connected units that could store a variety of dried cacao beans until needed in the production of chocolate. The silos were on the Dorchester side, between the Neponset River and River Street. The surface trolley on the right connected Ashmont Station and Mattapan and is listed in *Ripley's Believe It or Not* as the only trolley in the world to run through a cemetery, Cedar Grove Cemetery in Dorchester. *Courtesy of Andy Sawicky.*

The silos boldly advertised Baker Chocolate to all who passed by. Built in 1941, the silos were never filled to capacity, and after 1965, they stood forlorn and unused until their demolition in 1979.

The silos were built to hold tons of cacao beans. It was thought that World War II would impede the availability of cacao beans, and it was said that "there must be no shortage of chocolate, which is the chief essential of emergency rations for an army in the field." The silos, however, were never filled to capacity; still, they were an important and highly visible landmark of the complex, as they could be seen from all areas. In addition, they were adjacent to the railroad tracks and the surface trolley that connected Ashmont Station on the MBTA Red Line with Mattapan Station. The silos were abandoned by the early 1960s and demolished in 1987.

In the post–World War II era, the successful marketing by General Foods ensured that "Baker Chocolate" was a "trusted household name." Baker's was the oldest manufacturer of chocolate in the United States and was among the most respected and well-known producers in the food industry. General Foods was well aware that the Baker Division products had been used in American kitchens for generations, but it was only one of fourteen divisions with plants located in over fifty locations. During the 1950s, the Walter Baker Company, under the Jell-O Division, continued to produce cocoa, chocolate, an instant chocolate drink, Dream Whip and chocolate chips, as well as bulk chocolate and cocoas that were sold to the baking, ice cream and candy industries. Though profitable and well received locally, General Foods made the concerted decision in 1960 to consolidate the four plants operating under the Jell-O Division at a centralized facility, rather than continue at the scattered locations as they had for decades. These four divisions—the Walter Baker plant in Dorchester and Milton, Massachusetts; the Jell-O plant in New York; the Baker cocoanut plant in Hoboken, New Jersey; and the Minute Tapioca plant in Orange, Massachusetts—were by 1965 perceived by General Foods as "simply not efficient by current-day standards." Their consolidation in a central facility would allow for a single administrative organization, which, it was hoped, would prove to be as efficient as it was cost effective. The new consolidated plant was built in Dover, Delaware, and was opened in 1965.

Employees have always been an important part of the operation, since Nathaniel Blake was apprenticed to John Hannon. As Donald Blair said in 2006, "It was a great place to work, and they had some wonderful people working there, and I learned a lot from [older employees] as time went by."

WORLD WAR II

The Baker Chocolate Company saw many employees enlisting during World War II, and the company began to again produce chocolate rations for the soldiers and sailors serving in the war. The high caffeine content of the chocolate not only gave quick energy, but it was also a delicious and very welcome treat. In addition, the company, as a division of General Foods, contributed chocolate and cocoa to the war effort for food parcels distributed by the Red Cross to Allied war prisoners.

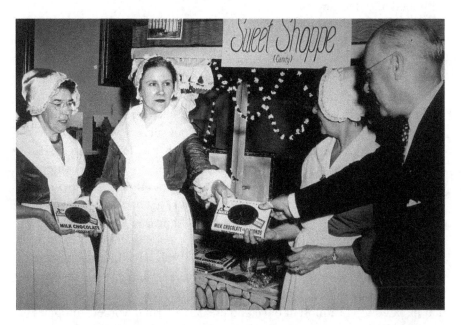

A trio of demonstrators offer bars of milk chocolate (some with almonds) at a "Sweet Shoppe" that was set up at the Second Church in Dorchester, the church where Walter Baker worshiped and to which he donated the tower clock.

THE GOLDEN AGE OF SNACK FOODS
A Quick, Delicious Snack that
Is Always Readily Available

By the twentieth century, chocolate had not only become a reliable and welcome snack food manufactured by companies established to produce chocolate bars, but it also was readily edible as well as delicious. Unlike Walter Baker & Company, Ltd., these competitive companies grew by leaps and bounds. The general public viewed these new chocolate confections as both food and delicacy.

In the twentieth century, especially between the two world wars, family meals became more rare and decidedly less formal, and the amount of snacking between meals increased as life became busier. With well-placed advertising and a wide array of chocolate snacks to choose from, the general public eagerly took to the new products, which combined delicious taste with nourishment and a quick form of energy. As a result, these new confectionary treats were enjoyed daily and were a tremendous success.

Beginning with the Hershey Company, which was founded in 1876 by Milton Snavely Hershey (1857–1945), many of these chocolate companies competed for the public's patronage of snack bars. After apprenticing as a confectioner in Philadelphia, Pennsylvania, Hershey had a tumultuous two decades of success and failure until he sold his Lancaster Caramel Company in 1900 and concentrated on making chocolate in a mill in his hometown of Derry Church, which was later renamed, in 1906, Hershey, Pennsylvania, in his honor. Hershey, reputedly with two workers hired from the Walter Baker & Company, Ltd. mills, manufactured milk chocolate so successfully that he saw success almost at once and created a virtual workers' utopia. His chocolate bars, made as early as 1894 and boldly embossed "Hershey," were a delicious and inexpensive way to snack. After 1907, they were augmented by a small, flat-bottomed, conically shaped dollop of milk chocolate that he

A pyramidal arrangement of cocoa tins, chocolate bars and glass jars that would be filled with chocolate bonbons was typical of the artistic displays set up by the demonstrators for exhibitions.

named "Hershey's Kisses." So successful were these silver foil–wrapped, one-bite chocolate kisses that they were patented and went on to become one of the most successful and well-known products of the Hershey Chocolate Company. In the following years, the company continued to be an innovative and creative manufacturer of chocolate, introducing new confections that included Sweethearts (1900), almond chocolate bars (1908), Mr. Goodbar (1925), Hershey's chocolate syrup (1926), chocolate chips (1928) and the Krackel bar (1938).

The Hershey Chocolate Company supplied the United States military with chocolate bars during World War II. These bars were called Ration D and Tropical bars. Ration D bars were developed as nonmelting, four-ounce chocolate bars with extra calories and vitamins that could be used as emergency provisions for soldiers and sailors. The Tropical bars were designed to not melt in warm weather, but while the attempts to retain the sweetened flavor were somewhat successful, many of the troops found the chocolate tough and unappetizing, and the bars were often said to resemble chocolate-flavored wax. Nevertheless, they were perfect as a quick snack in the field or as barter material. It is estimated that between 1940 and 1945, over 3 billion of the Ration D and Tropical bars were produced and distributed to soldiers throughout the world. In 1939, the Hershey plant was capable of producing an estimated 100,000 ration bars a day. By the end of World War II, the entire Hershey plant was producing ration bars at a rate of 24 million bars a week. The Hershey Chocolate Company was honored by the United States government with five Army-Navy "E" Production Awards for exceeding expectations for quality and quantity in the production of the Ration D and Tropical bars.

The Hershey Company plant in Hershey, Pennsylvania, today covers 2 million square feet of space and is reputedly the largest chocolate factory in the world. Hershey also has plants in Monterrey, Mexico, and in China. However, the success that Milton Hershey enjoyed after 1900, when he introduced his milk chocolate bar, was unprecedented and made his name synonymous with milk chocolate.

Another manufacturer of chocolate snack bars was the Mar-O-Bar Company, which was a candy company opened in 1911 by Franklin Clarence Mars (1883–1934) and Ethel Kissack Mars in Tacoma, Washington. Mars made the first Milky Way bars in 1923; these bars had a nougat center and saw immediate success. So successful was Mars that in 1929 he expanded his candy business by opening a plant in Chicago, Illinois, where, in 1930, he made the first Snickers candy bar, named after a beloved family horse.

Forrest E. Mars Sr. (1904–1999) was the son of the well-known candy makers, and following his graduation from Yale University, he began, in 1932, to make a decidedly different snack bar, which he called the Mars bar. After a rift with his father, he moved to Slough, Berkshire, in the United Kingdom, where he made his new candy bar; the snack was similar to his father's popular Milky Way, but his Mars bar had nougat *and* caramel covered in milk chocolate. This new candy bar was marketed throughout the United Kingdom and Europe and was widely successful. While living in England, Mars also bought the rights to Smarties, a popular sugar-coated chocolate candy. He returned to the United States in 1939 and went into partnership with R. Bruce Murrie (1854–1928), son of Hershey Chocolate Company president William F.R. Murrie, and they called their new chocolate company M&M Ltd. Their joint candy venture was located in Newark, New Jersey, and was to produce a small, circular disk of milk chocolate covered in a hard candy shell. They called these M&M's and marketed them as "melting in your mouth and not in your hand." It was said that Forrest Mars had visited Spain during its Civil War and saw soldiers eating small disks of chocolate that were protected from melting in their knapsacks or on their fingers by a hard candy shell coating. The new M&M's became very popular during World War II, when they were packed in cardboard tubes, shipped and included in the kits of soldiers and sailors with their food rations.

After World War II, the now popular M&M's, which were somewhat larger than they are now, were still sold in tubes and cost a nickel. The candy was originally made in five colors: brown, yellow, red, green and violet; in 1949, red was substituted for violet, but it was discontinued between 1976 and 1987 due to a scare surrounding the dye used for the color. After 1950, the brand name was reinforced by the capital letter M being stamped on each candy shell with a machine specially calibrated not to break the colored shell. M&M Ltd. was later merged with Mars, and the plant is today in McLean, Virginia, where the popular M&M's, Milky Way bars, Snickers bars and Three Musketeers bars are made.

The Hershey Chocolate Company, the Mar-O-Bar Company (later known as Mars) and M&M Ltd. were three of the many chocolate companies producing snack bars in the twentieth century. Among the other competitors were the Whitman Chocolate Company, which, in 1912, made and boxed what it marketed and sold as "Whitman's Samplers," marking the first instance of a company using a drawing on the inside lid to identify each of the different chocolates enclosed in the gift box. Other manufacturers were Otto J. Schoenleber (1858–1927), whose Ambrosia Chocolate Company in 1894 made bulk chocolate for large manufacturers such as Hostess, Pillsbury and Nabisco; Leo Hirschfeld (1869–1924), whose Sweets Company of America in 1896 made the first Tootsie Rolls, which he named after his daughter, Ellen "Tootsie" Hirschfield; L.S. Heath & Sons, Inc., which, in 1914, made the first Heath Bar and, in 1958, the Heath English Toffee Bar; Peter Paul Halijian (1850–1927), founder of the Peter Paul Candy Manufacturing Company, which, in 1921, made the first Mounds Candy Bar and, in 1946, the first Almond Joy Bar; and Harry Burnett Reese (1879–1856), who, in 1922, made the first Reese's Peanut Butter Cup using Hershey's milk chocolate; he also made what he called Johnny bars and Lizzy Bars. These snack bars were made in the United States but were among dozens of selections of eating chocolate that appealed to every palate.

Each of these chocolate companies had its ardent competitors and followers, but the chocolate products relied on people's weakness for sweets and their desire for filling and nutritious snacks.

LA BELLE CHOCOLATIERE

A Beautiful Chocolate Server
Who Became a Princess

Trademarks in the United States were an important way to have the public readily identify with a product or brand of food, but it was not until October 25, 1870, that the first trademark in this country was registered in the United States Patent Office. Known to be unofficially used before the Civil War by many companies, Walter Baker & Company initially employed a comely maiden with a cornucopia, from which Baker chocolate and cocoa products cascaded. However, it was Henry Lillie Pierce who adopted a beloved pastel portrait from the Gemaldegalerie alte Meister in Dresden, Germany, as his official trademark. It was registered in the patent office in 1881 and soon became one of the most identifiable trademarks in the food industry in the United States.

La Belle Chocolatiere is the official trademark of the Baker Chocolate Company. Though she has been used as the trademark of this delicious industry, La Belle was once an Austrian princess. In the mid-eighteenth century, chocolate shops were quite popular in Europe, and many fashionable people stopped into these shops for a cup of hot chocolate during the cold weather. La Belle, or Anna Baltauf (ca. 1740–1825), was the daughter of Melchior Baltauf, a knight of the Austrian court, and lived in Vienna. The fact that she was a chocolate server has never been fully explained or understood, but whether she was earning wages as a chocolate server or did it as a lark, she was said to have met her future husband one cold winter afternoon in 1760.

The story, as related to Henry Lillie Pierce, was that Anna Baltauf was serving chocolate in a shop in Vienna one afternoon when Dietrichstein, a prince of the Austrian Empire, entered for a cup of hot chocolate. Serving the cup of chocolate with a glass of water, Anna captivated the prince with

Das Schokoladenmadchen is a portrait by Jean-Etienne Liotard of Anna Baltauf as a chocolate server in Vienna in 1765. Henry Lillie Pierce had this pastel portrait copied and renamed *La Belle Chocolatiere.* Since 1883, La Belle Chocolatiere has been the trademark of Walter Baker & Company. *Courtesy of Staatliche Kunstsammlungen, Dresden.*

her beauty, and their courtship culminated in marriage. On her wedding day, Anna was quoted as saying to her fellow chocolate bearers, "Behold! Now that I am a princess you may kiss my hand." Prince Dietrichstein, to capture and preserve his consort's beauty, had her portrait painted in the costume in which he had first met her. The artist, Jean-Etienne Liotard (1702–1790) was in Vienna at that time as painter to the court. He had recently completed portraits of the Empress Maria Theresa and other members of the imperial family and court, but this painting of Anna was probably one of the most charming of his portraits. Anna, however, lived an uneventful life after her courtship and marriage and died in Vienna in 1825.

The portrait, which hangs in the Royal Portrait Collection of the Dresden Gallery in Dresden, Germany, was seen by Henry Lillie Pierce in 1862 on one of his many trips to Europe. Taken by the likeness, and by the appropriate fact that the subject was a chocolate server, Pierce requested that a copy be made for the Baker Chocolate Company offices in Dorchester. The copy, a large, full-length canvas, was shipped to this country and installed in the Pierce office. By 1872, La Belle had become the trademark of the oldest chocolate manufacturer in this country, whose product would be known throughout the world for being a "perfect food, as wholesome as delicious, a beneficent restorer of exhausted power."

Pierce, like the Baker family before him, extolled the virtues of chocolate as nourishing and easily digestible, as well as a delicious beverage when made properly. Baker's Chocolate advertisements during the mid- and late

A young demonstrator poses in 1904 as she frosts a chocolate cake with chocolate frosting, all made from the *Choice Recipes* cookbooks, which were available gratis to the public.

nineteenth century said that its chocolate "soothes both stomach and brain, and for this reason, as well as for others, it is the best friend of those engaged in literary pursuits."

The demonstrators, comely young women who dressed as the trademark come to life, were an important part of the workforce in the late nineteenth and early twentieth centuries. These women wore brown silk dresses with aprons, bonnets and sashes in fine white linen, as well as gloves. The A.W. Tams Company of 318 West Forty-sixth Street in New York City made many of these demonstrator costumes, which were individually boxed in leather cases so the women could travel from venue to venue with their outfits. According to Margaret S. MacGillivary, former secretary of Henry Lillie Pierce, in 1893 the costumes of the demonstrators were made by a "fashionable dress-making house on Boylston St. [in Boston], at a cost of $80.00 per girl. This included waist of gold satin, skirt of blue taffeta silk, cap of silk trimmed with lace." The cost was tremendous considering that employees earned twelve dollars per week on average in 1900. Miss MacGillivary commissioned C.F. Hovey & Company on Summer Street in Boston to make the linen parts of the costumes, which "cut down the expense of these costumes tremendously."

Today, the pastel portrait of *Das Schokoladenmadchen* can be admired at the Gemaldegalerie alte Meister in Dresden, Germany.

EMPLOYEES AND ASSOCIATES

Everyone seemed to think Bakers was a good company to work for.
—*Karen Mac Nutt*

Not only was the Baker Chocolate Company in the Lower Mills/Milton Village the oldest manufacturer of chocolate in the United States, founded in 1765 and established in 1780, but it was also one of the first large companies in this country to establish and annually contribute to a profit-sharing plan for the benefit of its employees.

Profit-sharing plans, as well as 401(k) plans, are one of the many enticements used to retain key employees who make substantial contributions to the operation of a company. A plan that gives employees a share of the profits of the company is a great way to instill a sense of ownership and thereby extract high expectations and hopefully lengthy service from them. However, in 1904 the Forbes Syndicate, which had purchased the profitable chocolate company in 1897 for $4.75 million from the estate of Henry L. Pierce, gave a week's salary to four hundred employees of the chocolate mills with one year or more of service as extra compensation.

In 1905, the Baker Chocolate Company was quoted by the *Boston Transcript*, a leading newspaper of the day, in a letter to employees:

> *The directors of Walter Baker & Co. Limited, are pleased to be able to enclose with your pay this week a check the amount of which is based on the number of days' service in employ of the company during the last year. It is recognized by the company that your personal efforts and interest will insure the continued high quality of our product, thus making our business success permanent.*

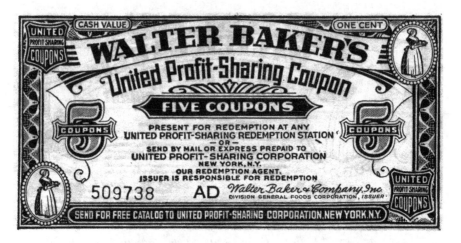

Walter Baker & Company, Ltd., offered United profit-sharing coupons that could be redeemed by employees for merchandise through a catalogue provided by a redemption center in New York.

The article went on to say that "the company showed its interest in the welfare of its people last week by enclosing in the envelope of each employee a check for an amount of money equal to ten percent of his or her earnings during 1904."

A 10 percent profit-sharing check is a substantial one, but more importantly, it reflected that company management sincerely recognized employees as a vital part of Baker Chocolate Company's success. Shortly thereafter, further incentives were instituted. In 1909, the management reduced the fifty-eight-hour work week to fifty-six hours. In 1916, an eight-hour workday was instituted, with time and a half for extra hours. In 1922, cooperative group life insurance plans were offered to employees. In 1934, a cooperative retirement plan for employees was established. In 1936, a vacation with pay plan was established, and in 1937, a sickness benefit plan was put in place.

All in all, a job at the Baker Chocolate Company was not just something that was appreciated and rewarded by the management, but it was also a decidedly delicious one.

SAMUEL GERMAN

Samuel German (1802–1888), or "Sammy," as he was often called, came from Biddeford, Devonshire, England, to Dorchester, Massachusetts, to work for Thomas Tremlett, whose estate was at the corner of Washington and

Tremlett Streets, just north of Codman Square. German married Charlotte P. Dyer of Franklin, Maine, and lived on Baker's Court in Dorchester Lower Mills. Thomas Tremlett was also an Englishman by birth, and German did odd jobs for him. Within a few years, German had become acquainted with Walter Baker, whose estate adjoined Tremlett's. By 1840, German was employed as Baker's coachman, but shortly thereafter, he took a job at the chocolate mill. By 1852, he had perfected a new chocolate that was called German's Sweet Chocolate. This recipe, which had a higher content of sugar than Baker's Premium No. 1, was said to be "palatable, nutritious and healthful, and is a great favorite with children." Walter Baker bought the recipe from Sammy German for $1,000 and began marketing it as "Baker's German Sweet Chocolate."

A century after Samuel German created his sweet chocolate, a recipe for German Chocolate Cake appeared as the "Recipe of the Day" in the June 3, 1957 edition of the *Dallas Morning Star*. The column, written by Julie Benell, food editor of the newspaper, stated that the premise was for "something borrowed" recipes and that the chocolate cake recipe was sent in by Mrs. George Clay of 3831 Academy Drive, Dallas, Texas. However, the column of June 3, 1957, contained an error in the recipe, saying that

Samuel German produced German's Sweet Chocolate, a sweet chocolate that could be eaten as well as used in baking. German is buried at Cedar Grove Cemetery in Dorchester.

the recipe called for an eight-ounce bar of melted German Sweet Chocolate. The June 5, 1957 "Recipe of the Day" column carried a correction, stating that a four-ounce bar of chocolate should be used, rather than an eight-ounce bar. Additionally, the August 21, 1957 column, which repeated the recipe, called for a quarter-ounce bar. Whatever the correct amount, it seemed that the result was a deliciously rich and flavorful chocolate cake.

In 1958, an article appeared in the *Dallas Morning News* stating that General Foods was making the recipe for German Chocolate Cake available in a recipe booklet. The article stated that, while Mrs. Clay's recipe was the first to appear in the paper, "Mrs. Jackie Huffines, Dallas County food conservationist, had sent a chocolate cake made with a similar

Samuel German Chocolate Cake

4 ounces Baker's German Sweet Chocolate
1 cup unsalted butter, room temperature, divided
¼ cup warm milk
2½ cups cake flour, sifted
1 teaspoon baking soda
½ teaspoon sea salt
5 medium egg whites
2 cups sugar
5 medium egg yolks
1 teaspoon pure vanilla extract
¾ cup buttermilk

For the coconut-pecan frosting:
1 cup sugar
4 egg yolks
1 cup evaporated milk
½ cup unsalted butter
1 teaspoon pure vanilla extract
10 ounces coconut, freshly grated
1½ cups pecans, finely ground

Prepare the chocolate by melting it in the top of a double boiler (or microwave), stirring until smooth. Add ¼ cup of the butter and stir until it is melted and blended. Add warm milk and stir until smooth. Let the chocolate cool. Preheat the oven to 350 degrees.

Grease the bottoms only of three nine-inch cake pans with solid shortening and dust lightly with flour. Sift together the flour, baking soda and salt. Whip the egg whites until stiff using the wire beater of a mixer. Transfer the beaten egg whites to a separate bowl and set aside.

In the mixer bowl, cream the remaining ¾ cup butter and sugar. Add the egg yolks one at a time, beating well after each addition. Add the melted, cooled chocolate and the vanilla. Mix well.

With the mixer on very low, stir in the flour mixture alternately with the buttermilk. Scrape the sides and bottom of the bowl and stir again. With a long-handled spatula, fold and stir the beaten egg whites into the batter until the batter is smooth.

Divide the batter evenly between the prepared pans and bake for thirty-five minutes on the middle rack of the oven. The cake is done when it begins to pull away from the sides of the pans and springs back to a light touch. Cool layers in the pans for about ten minutes, and then run a knife around the edges of each pan and turn the layers out onto wire racks that have been sprayed with cooking spray. Cool layers completely before frosting.

To make the frosting, combine the sugar, egg yolks and evaporated milk in the top of a double boiler. Stir with a wire whisk until the yolks are fully incorporated and add the butter. Place over simmering water and bring to a boil. Simmer for fifteen minutes, stirring constantly, until the mixture thickens. Add the vanilla, coconut and nuts and cool.

To assemble the cake, place one layer on a cake stand and spread with frosting. Frost each layer completely, top and sides, as it is added to the cake. Enjoy!

WALTER BAKER & CO'S
GERMAN'S
SWEET CHOCOLATE

FAC-SIMILE ¼ LB. PACKAGE.

Left: A bar of German's Sweet Chocolate was wrapped in a polychromatic paper marked "formula of S. German, Dorchester, Mass.," with printed directions on how to properly melt it in boiling water and then enjoy.

Below: Jane Schroth (left) and Anne Melanson pose on either side of a display of Walter Baker's Farmington Chocolate, which was advertised as "a treat to eat." This display was at Preston's Market, owned by James and Grace Roberts, on Adams Street in Milton Village. *Courtesy of Jane Schroth Lemire.*

recipe to Miss Benell's television kitchen, where it was shown to homemakers on her daily program."

Thus, with a delicious tradition begun in 1852 by Samuel German, the sweet chocolate was enhanced a century later with a new and delicious tradition: German Chocolate Cake. The recipe on page 82, if followed closely, will allow your family and friends to taste how truly delicious this cake really is!

SIDNEY B. WILLIAMS

Sidney Williams (1795–1854) was the son of Robert Williams, a successful and wealthy East India merchant from Boston. The Williams family moved to Philadelphia, Pennsylvania, in the 1830s, and in 1840, Walter Baker married Sidney's sister, Eleanor Jameson Williams, in Philadelphia. Williams was employed by a Mr. Smith but was induced by Walter Baker to come to work for him after his late wife's brother, John P. Mott, deserted him and, as he said, "imposed upon me more writing & labor than I can conveniently attend to." Williams came to work for his brother-in-law in 1843, as his work in Philadelphia was said to be "extremely dull." Williams served as Walter Baker's personal clerk but was also taught the business so he could manage it when Baker was not present. The arrangement was formalized in an agreement that provided for Williams's livelihood, which increased over five years with one-third of the profits after Walter Baker's retirement. This agreement, obviously drafted by Walter Baker, who had studied at the law school of Judge Tappan Reeves, stated that if Williams ever left to commence his own chocolate business (as others had previously done), he would pay $15,000 to Walter Baker as legal damages.

In 1852, upon the death of Walter Baker, Williams assumed full control of the chocolate mill when the trustees of the Baker Estate leased the business to him. He continued the business under the old name of Walter Baker & Company, with Henry L. Pierce as head of the countingroom at South Market Street in Quincy Market, Boston. Sidney Williams unfortunately died two years later on a business trip to Montreal, Canada, and the trustees of the Baker Estate then leased the business to Henry L. Pierce for a two-year trial period.

NATHANIEL JEREMIAH BRADLEE

Nathaniel J. Bradlee (1829–1888) was born in Boston, the son of Samuel and Elisabeth Davis Williams Bradlee. Educated at the Chauncey Hall School in Boston, he was later apprenticed to George Minot Dexter, a prominent Boston architect, with whom he remained and to whose architectural practice he succeeded in 1856. Throughout the next three decades, Bradlee designed such prominent buildings as the Danvers Insane Asylum, the New England and Union Life Insurance Companies, the Waterworks in Chestnut Hill, the Young Men's Christian Union and numerous banks and residences in Boston.

Nathaniel J. Bradlee was an architect who was engaged to design the Pierce Mill by Henry L. Pierce, president of Walter Baker & Company. Seen here are, from the left, Anna M. Vose, holding Helen Curtis Bradlee; Eleanor Bradlee; Nathaniel Bradlee; and Julia Weld Bradlee. Bradlee, later with his associates Winslow and Wetherell, would design the mills until 1919, when the Administration Building was designed by George F. Shepard. *Courtesy of Judith R.E. Bullock.*

It was Bradlee who designed the important architectural prototype of the red brick row house that was built throughout the new South End of Boston, an area created on either side of "The Neck," the narrow strip of land that connected Boston to the mainland at Roxbury. His prototype design was composed of red brick, swell-bay façade row houses, with mansard roofs and steep front stairs that shared common setback, height and building materials and created both a uniform and urbane streetscape that made the new South End of Boston the premier residential district of the city at the time of the Civil War.

In the early 1870s, Bradlee was commissioned by Henry Lillie Pierce to design a new mill to be built on Adams Street in Dorchester Lower Mills. This mill, built in 1872, was a large, French Second Empire design that utilized red brick, with brownstone lintels and a fashionable mansard roof with iron cresting. Named for Pierce, it created an impressive approach to the Lower Mills, which was seen from all directions, and its successful design led to further commissions from Pierce that continued to Bradlee's successors, Winslow and Wetherell.

Bradlee was a resident of Roxbury, Massachusetts, where his elegant estate had an impressive columned Greek Revival mansion, greenhouses, parterres of fruit trees and a six-story observatory, from which panoramic views were unparalleled. In the 1870s, after Roxbury had been annexed to the city of Boston in 1868, Bradlee began subdividing his estate and building speculative row housing that transformed the area into an elegant Victorian neighborhood. He was instrumental in bringing water to the city from Lake Cochituate, and his service on the city's water board led to the construction of a reservoir and waterworks on Chestnut Hill; he was the architect of the waterworks building. Active in city politics, a noteworthy trustee of estates and a committed citizen of the city, he not only benefited his fellow residents through the introduction of pure water but also transformed the city architecturally.

ELLEN SWALLOW RICHARDS

Ellen S. Richards (1842–1911) graduated from Vassar College and became the first female student at the Massachusetts Institute of Technology in Boston. She specialized in environmental studies and is considered the founder of home economics. The National Women's Hall of Fame inducted her into its hallowed halls in 1993 and, in so honoring her, said:

WALTER BAKER & CO'S
COCOA AND CHOCOLATE

Can always be depended upon by cooks, caterers, and physicians to produce uniform results because they are of uniform quality, of high grade, and absolutely pure.
Be sure that you get the genuine goods bearing our trade-mark.

WALTER BAKER & CO. Ltd., Dorchester, Mass.

In an advertisement from 1900, a young girl grates a chocolate bar to make cocoa, with a tray bearing cocoa cups and a cocoa pot awaiting the delicious drink. One could always depend on Baker's to "produce uniform results because they are of uniform quality, of high grade, and absolutely pure."

Ellen Swallow Richards was the first woman professional chemist in the nation, and played a major role to open scientific education and the scientific professions to women. She was the first scientist to conduct stream by stream water surveys in the United States. By applying scientific principles to domestic life, she was to pioneer the new study and profession of home economics, a major opportunity at the time for higher education and employment for American women.

Ellen Richards was the first woman to study, and eventually to be graduated, at the Massachusetts Institute of Technology, and she went on to develop MIT's Women's Laboratory. Her innovative and highly impactive studies of air, water and food led to the creation of national public health standards and the new disciplines of sanitary engineering and nutrition; she demonstrated the need for Massachusetts factory and food inspection laws, which were the very first in the United States. The interaction between people and their environment led this dedicated visionary to predict future environmental crises and to advance the concept of ecology as an environmental science, an idea not widely accepted until almost a century passed. Richards was central to the founding of the American Home Economics Association and served as the group's first president.

Along with women such as Maria Parloa, Janet McKenzie Hill, Elizabeth Kevill Burr, A. Louise Andrea and even the famous author of the *Boston Cooking School Cookbook*, Fannie Merritt Farmer, Ellen Swallow Richards offered suggestions about the cooking of chocolate and cocoa in almost every cookbook published by Walter Baker & Company, Ltd., in the early twentieth century. As a person knowledgeable about chocolate, she extolled its virtues as a pure and wholesome food, and in her writings, she said:

> *In preparing* [cocoa] *as a beverage for the table a mistake has been frequently made in considering chocolate merely as a flavor, an adjunct to the rest of the meal, instead of giving it its due prominence as a real food, containing all the necessary nutritive principles. A cup of chocolate made with sugar and milk is in itself a fair breakfast.*

Even Dr. Edwin Lankester, an English surgeon and naturalist who made great strides to stem the spread of cholera in London, was quoted as saying that cocoa contained as much flesh-forming matter as beef!

MARIA PARLOA

Maria Parloa (1843–1909) was a native Bostonian who became a noted spokesperson for the Walter Baker & Company, Ltd. Miss Parloa, as she was known to many readers, began her career as a cook, working at one point as the pastry cook at the famous Appledore House on Appledore Island off the New Hampshire Coast, immortalized by Celia Thaxter, whose family operated the famous inn for decades. Thaxter's 1872 book, *The Appledore Cook Book*, included her recipe for tomato chowder, which is still credited as the first tomato soup recipe to appear in print. After Parloa's graduation from the Maine Central Institute in 1871, she relocated in the winters to Mandarin, Florida, where she began offering cooking classes that were fully subscribed and launched her eventual career as a cooking teacher.

Miss Parloa returned to Boston, where she taught domestic science at the Lasell (now College) Female Seminary in Newton, Massachusetts, which was founded in 1851 by Edward Lasell. Her astute teaching methods were well received, and she opened Miss Parloa's Cooking School on Tremont Street in Boston. This led to her teaching at the Boston Cooking School, which she is also credited with cofounding. Parloa expanded her cooking school to New York City, where she offered classes for enrolled students during the day and free classes in the evening for immigrant women, who learned how to prepare highly nutritious but also economical meals for their families. Relocating in 1887 back to Boston, for the next two decades she had a very productive and financially successful career. Her partial ownership of the *Ladies Home Journal* magazine allowed her articles on food and its preparation to be read by women far and wide, and her cookbooks, beginning in 1878

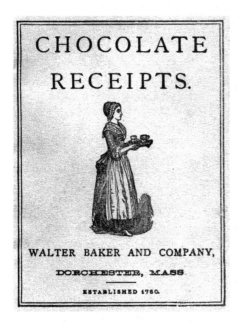

CHOCOLATE RECEIPTS.

WALTER BAKER AND COMPANY,

DORCHESTER, MASS.

ESTABLISHED 1760.

An early cookbook published by Walter Baker & Company was called *Chocolate Receipts* and instructed one on how to properly melt chocolate and combine it with other ingredients to enjoy as cocoa or as a dessert.

with *Camp Cookery*, eventually numbered eleven, including *Miss Parloa's New Cook Book: A Guide to Marketing* and *Cooking and Chocolate and Cocoa Recipes by Miss Parloa* for the Walter Baker & Company.

Miss Parloa extolled the nutritional qualities of chocolate, and her articles and recipes were well received by a chocolate-loving readership. Her interest in the science of cooking, and her friendships with Ellen Swallow Richards, Mary Bailey Lincoln and Fannie Farmer, expended her culinary interests, cooking skills and ability to teach others the skills and joys of cooking. Her innovative cooking skills led to a recipe in her 1882 book *Miss Parloa's New Cookbook* for "Pigs-in-a-Blanket," fresh oysters seasoned with salt and pepper, rolled in a slice of bacon, secured with a toothpick and broiled, and then served hot on toast. This highly innovative cook was also able to master the many skills necessary to teach the public to cook with ease and skill, and Walter Baker & Company continued to solicit her input and involvement until her death in 1909 in Bethel, Connecticut.

HUGH MCCUE

Hugh McCue (1861–1948) was born in Dorchester, Massachusetts, but his family moved to Milton shortly thereafter. He graduated from Milton High School and was employed at Walter Baker & Company for forty-six years, beginning in 1887. He reminisced in 1940 about his career at the company and said that previous to his employment, he

was a stone cutter by trade, and so became useful in the care of the mills, which at that time were great cumbersome affairs of granite about five feet in diameter set on the floor with heavy timbers to support them. They became smooth from constant grinding, and had to be taken up and dressed quite frequently. To do this, three or four men were required to re-surface them with small steel picks. I introduced the bush-hammer, which is used in stone cutting, and it did the work better and much quicker.

He continued:

Sometime previous to 1900, I was put in charge of the old Preston Mill, which was run by two tub water wheels. I kept an accurate record of what I did, and they never knew just how much dust they made until I turned in my account. They made a preparation called Webb's Cocoa Powder out of it and sold it, thus getting some revenue from this by-product. In 1902, Mr. Gallagher put me in charge of the new Ware Mill, where I remained until I was pensioned. My job was a little different from the rest of the foremen's as they mostly had charge of one operation, but in my small mill I had charge of the whole thing from the raw cocoa to the finished product. Consequently, when they started the mill in Montreal, I went up there with Mr. Thurber...and Mr. Gallagher [and made three trips to instruct in the manufacturing of liquors from the raw cacao bean], *and continued to go up there for some years thereafter, as became necessary.*

DR. CARLTON A. ROWE

Carlton Rowe (1882–1961) was born in Fitzwilliam, New Hampshire, and graduated from the Tufts Medical School in Boston. During World War I, he served as a captain in the American Medical Corps in France. Dr. Rowe and his wife, Blanche Lord Rowe, came to Milton, Massachusetts, in 1908 and purchased 454 Adams Street in East Milton. Active in the community and at the Second Congregational Church (now known as the East Milton Congregational Church), it was Dr. Rowe who successfully petitioned the trustees of the Cunningham Foundation to lay out tennis courts at Cunningham Park in East Milton, where he established the first tennis club in town.

Associated with the Milton Convalescent Home, later to be renamed the Milton Hospital and located at the former Cunningham Estate on Edge Hill Road, he succeeded Dr. M. Vassar Pierce as chief of staff in 1932. Since 1904, the convalescent home had offered medical care to the people

1840 - Doctors now recommend
Baker's Chocolate
as a "beneficent restorer of exhausted power"

A perfect food, preserves health, prolongs life, soothes both stomach and brain.

In the *Calendar of Fashions*, published in 1900 by Walter Baker & Company, Ltd, it boldly stated that doctors recommend Baker's Chocolate as a "beneficent restorer of exhausted power" and that it is "a perfect food, preserves health, prolongs life, soothes both stomach and brain."

of Milton, from maternity care to convalescence. In the late 1940s, Milton Hospital purchased from the Pierce heirs Fair Oaks, the large summer estate of Wallace Lincoln Pierce that had been designed by William Ralph Emerson and originally built for railroad magnate Albert E. Touzelin. The house was demolished, and in 1950, Joseph Daniels Leland of the Boston architectural firm Leland & Larson designed the new Milton Hospital. Acting as "clerk of the works" was Dr. Rowe, who must have, with justifiable pride, seen the new modern hospital as the capstone of his long and eminently successful association with the Milton Hospital.

Dr. Rowe was also the medical director of the Walter Baker Hospital, which was located in the Webb Mill (designed by Bradlee & Winslow and built in 1882) at the corner of Adams and Eliot Streets in Milton Village). The Webb Mill was named for the former Webb & Twombley Chocolate Company, which had been a rival of Baker Chocolate from 1843 to 1881. Established in 1924 with a registered nurse in charge of the hospital, Dr. Carlton Rowe was, according to his obituary, "instrumental in developing an outstanding medical department which has been cited by the American College of Surgeons for its accomplishments in the field of industrial medicines." While Dr. Rowe served as medical director, he worked with Curtis H. Gager, president of Baker Chocolate since 1936, to maintain the aspect of healthy, and thereby happy, employees at the company.

In 1958, following his retirement, Dr. Rowe and his wife retired to Norway, Maine. Though for the last three years of his life he lived away from Milton, his accomplishments and obvious concern for his patients are remembered long after his death.

CLARA PINCKNEY

Clara Sophia Brown Pinckney (1856–1953) was the daughter of Abraham and Alice Durkee Pinckney and was raised in Yarmouth, Nova Scotia. She came to Dorchester in 1878, living on Washington Street in the Lower Mills.

Miss Pinckney was initially working in the dry goods store of E.E. Wendemuth in Milton Village, but after a brief course in stenography, she was employed in 1892 as the first woman stenographer at Baker Chocolate and remained the only such employee for the next fifteen years. In 1919, when the new Administration Building was completed, the factory office force and the office force from Boston moved into new offices on April 20, 1919. Miss Pinckney was given a private office on the second-floor front and remained there for thirty-seven years, until her retirement in 1929. A dutiful and dedicated employee, and a close family friend of Hugh Clifford Gallagher and his wife, Miss Pinckney said in 1940 that she could not "remember in my time that any special effort was made to manufacture new products. Their line was well known, and, of course, at that time, there was not the strong competition which exists today." The office staff increased steadily so that by 1940, only five decades after she was first employed, there were "about one hundred young women employed in the office building." Her memories of the business were summed up in 1940 in a poignant line in which she said more than she might have realized: "All so changed and so big now."

GEORGE F. SHEPARD JR.
Administration Building

The Administration Building was designed by George F. Shepard Jr. (1865–1955), partner with Frederick Baldwin Stearns of the prestigious Boston architectural firm of Shepard & Stearns. A native Miltonian, and son of local builder George F. Shepard (1827–1908), Shepard built his first home on Cliff Road—a large Shingle-style house. He later built his retirement home at 125 Canton Avenue. Shepard was also the architect of *Winter Valley*, the Geoffrey W. Whitney Estate, the Milton Woman's Clubhouse and the Colicott and Cunningham Schools in Milton. In the design of the Baker Administration Building, Shepard used red brick, which united the building with the other mills; however, it was designed as a Classical Georgian Revival building with four monumental façade Ionic columns, a roof balustrade and limestone trim. This was the first building in the mill complex that was not designed by Bradlee, Winslow & Wetherell or its successors, and it was in marked architectural contrast to those mills built between 1872 and 1918.

Shepard designed an impressive classical entry of white marble, with a flight of white marble stairs flanked by elegant bronze balustrades that led to a second-floor landing. At the top of the staircase, between flanking pilasters, he designed a panel for the life-sized oil portrait of La Belle Chocolatiere that was commissioned from the noted Boston School artist Howard B. Smith. When the portrait, a copy of *Das Schokoladenmadchen*, was installed in 1920, it was "considered by those who have seen it as the finest reproduction of La Belle Chocolatiere, the widely known Walter Baker & Company trademark that has ever been painted." The portrait was not only an impressive work of art but also a larger-than-life trademark and an important part of the company's history.

Howard B. Smith was "considered one of the most successful among Boston portrait painters," and company officials, employees and visitors to the Baker Administration Building for the next four decades were suitably impressed. After Walter Baker & Company moved to Dover, Delaware, in 1966, the Administration Building was used for various purposes, including as the local office of the Commonwealth's Department of Welfare. Covered over for many years after the building was abandoned, the portrait has once again become the focus of the renovation of the Baker Administration Building for artists' lofts, community space and the long hoped for museum of the Baker Chocolate Company. At its ribbon-cutting ceremony in October 2002, at which Senator Brian Joyce officiated, numerous elected officials, community activists and members of the general public saw the beginnings of the long-awaited restorations.

JANE SCHROTH LEMIRE

Jane Schroth Lemire is the daughter of Walter Schroth, quality-control manager at Baker Chocolate for many years. Employed before her marriage as a demonstrator, she extolled the virtues of poise and charm.

These mid-twentieth-century demonstrators had the pleasant task of going out as the marketing agents for the Walter Baker Division of General Foods. Along with her friend Anne Melanson and others, Schroth went to various stores to market new varieties of chocolate dressed as the company trademark La Belle Chocolatiere. The friends would pose on either side of a

Left: Jane Schroth was considered among "the foxiest" of the chocolate girls. Jane Schroth's father was Walter Schroth, a quality-control manager at Baker Chocolate for many years. *Courtesy of Jane Schroth Lemire.*

Below: Presenting a 1954 Ford convertible for a raffle to benefit Dorchester Day are, from the left, Stephen Burke, Walter Baker Company director of public relations; Senator William J. Keenan, Variety Show chairman; Leo Murphy, Dorchester Day general chairman; and Clifford Spiller, general manager of Walter Baker Chocolate and Cocoa. The Baker's Chocolate girls are Lorraine Naples, Jane Schroth and Ruth Stelberger. The car was awarded as a door prize at the Variety Show at the Riverview Ballroom on June 7, 1954. The car was purchased from the Stilphen Motor Company at 370 Columbia Road in Dorchester, a local Ford dealer. *Courtesy of Jane Schroth Lemire.*

display of such things as Walter Baker's Farmington Chocolate, which was advertised as "a treat to eat." They would set up displays with free samples at First National Market in the Lower Mills, the A&P in Codman Square and at Preston's Market in Milton Village, which was owned by James and Grace Roberts. (James was a nephew of Henry Lillie Pierce.)

Among the myriad activities that Jane Schroth and her coworkers undertook on behalf of the company was to help in the advertisement of such things as a Variety Show sponsored by the Dorchester Day Celebrations Committee in June 1954. This dinner dance, which was held at the Riverview Ballroom, part of the Winter Garden Rollerway, was located at 726 Gallivan Boulevard in Dorchester, where the off ramp from the Southeast Expressway is now located. This gala event was attended by the demonstrators, and a raffle was held with the grand door prize of a Ford convertible that had been donated by the Stilphen Motor Company near Upham's Corner in Dorchester. This was an important and exciting way that Baker Chocolate participated in community events and thereby ensured not only that its company was well known locally but also that its product was the chocolate of choice.

HAZEL STONE STANLEY

Hazel Stone Stanley (1903–1972) was born in Peabody, Massachusetts. Orphaned as a baby, she eventually lived with her sister, Sarah Stone Simpson, and her family near Adams Village in Dorchester. Sarah Simpson was employed at Baker Chocolate as a chocolate maker, and her husband, Willard Simpson, was employed at Mason Regulator Company in the Lower Mills, so it was natural that Hazel would seek employment at the company. As her niece Karen Mac Nutt said, "Everyone seemed to think Baker's was a good company to work for."

Hazel and her husband, Walter Stanley, both worked at Baker Chocolate; she filled cocoa tins and he worked in the silos with the cacao beans. It was a good job, with fair pay, and the conditions were good. Sarah Simpson "often commented on how clean things were required to be" at the plant. The pervasive aroma of chocolate was always there. However, Hazel recalled that the company's "rule about eating chocolate was the same for all employees. You could eat all you want, but you could not take any home. After a short while, the people who worked there had little interest in eating chocolate."

Walter Stanley worked as a foreman at the silos, and after forty years of service he retired in 1965. Hazel also worked at Baker Chocolate until her retirement in

Hazel Stone Stanley demonstrates the filling of cocoa tins on a conveyor belt to Curtis H. Gager, president of the Baker Division of General Foods. Mrs. Stanley received a production award, which recognized her conscientious work at the company. *Courtesy of Karen L. Mac Nutt.*

1968. She was recognized for her efficiency and swiftness in filling cocoa tins on a conveyor belt, receiving an award from Curtis Gager, president of the Baker Division of General Foods. Her sister Sarah was also "honored as one of Baker's best workers," and this recognition was a way of not only showing the company's appreciation but also of rewarding their efforts. In fact, at "Christmas they always gave the employees a gift, usually food." Hazel's niece remembers "a bell, a picnic basket, and a jewelry box, among other things."

The extended Stone-Stanley-Mac Nutt family was typical of Baker Chocolate workers. They were instrumental in making the operations run smoothly and swiftly, and their efforts were appreciated by the company. In fact, after World War II, when Willard Simpson returned home, "someone else had his job." Rather than turning away a loyal employee who had served in the war, Baker Chocolate found him a job—that "of raising and lowering the flag every day at his former rate of pay" until a suitable job utilizing his skills was found. This sense of benevolence and fairness ensured loyalty by employees who had long years of service.

DONALD AGNETTA

Donald Agnetta was born in Dorchester Lower Mills, Massachusetts, in 1936, the son of the late Daniel and Mildred Willard Agnetta. As a student at Boston College, he applied for work at the Baker Chocolate Company's Administration Building and was hired in the summer of 1954. He was hired to clean the small chocolate tank cars, filled with liquid chocolate, that traveled from the Park Mill to other mills in the complex. His job was to use a scraper to dislodge the solidified chocolate as best he could and then use hot water to melt the chocolate and wash away the residue from the interior of the tank. In addition to this job, he would also operate the conch machine, which mixed chocolate before it was cooled and hardened. These machines usually had four workers, with rotating shifts covering twenty-four hours a day, seven days a week, on three time schedules: 8:00 a.m. to 4:00 p.m., 4:00 p.m. to midnight and midnight to 8:00 a.m. The latter two shifts had a ten-cent-per-hour differential from the day shift, which he was gently induced to trade by the married men in his crew. Many employees lived within walking distance of the mills in Dorchester and Milton, but others came by public transportation. Baker Chocolate was a "great employer and after the Quincy Shipyard the biggest employer on the South Shore at the time."

Working in the summer months of June, July and August, it was a necessary but dirty job. The small tank cars were only used within the mill complex and were roughly one-twelfth the size of the large tank cars that held liquid chocolate and were shipped on the railroad. The aroma of chocolate creates a romantic and delicious concept, but Agnetta and neighbors of the chocolate mills often felt it was somewhat overpowering. Once he went into Boston with a friend to enjoy a drink at a bar. Two women were seated near them, and one woman turned to her friend and said, quizzically, "I smell chocolate." Her friend turned and looked at Agnetta and said that it was the two men seated at the bar. Thanks to the heavenly aroma of Baker's Chocolate, a conversation was started!

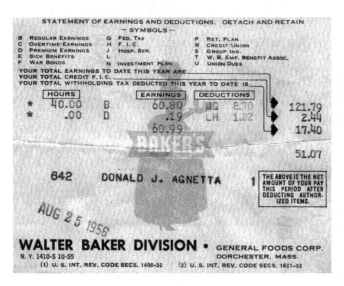

The August 25, 1956 payroll statement of summer employee Donald J. Agnetta. *Courtesy of Donald J. Agnetta.*

Donald Agnetta enjoyed his summer work at Baker Chocolate, but one month following his graduation from Boston College, he entered the United States military service and had no plans on reentering the workforce. He became an educator in the Boston Public Schools.

BAKER CHOCOLATE WORLD WAR II MEMORIAL

In 1948, the Baker Chocolate Company and the Federal Labor Union No. 21243 of Dorchester Lower Mills, affiliated with the American Federation of Labor, erected a large granite monument at Cedar Grove Cemetery in Dorchester in memory of seven employees who died in service during World War II. The monument, set in a small garden circle, is inscribed "In Memory of Walter Baker Men and Women Who Served in World War II and Dedicated to Those Who Made the Supreme Sacrifice."

The seven men who were employees of Baker Chocolate and died during the war were remembered on Memorial Day, May 30, 1948, when the monument was dedicated. They were:

William J. Caddy
Matthew R. Curran
John J. Gallagher
Richard E. La Farge

Alfred J. Matthews
Stephen L. Sullivan Jr.
G. Fred Willard

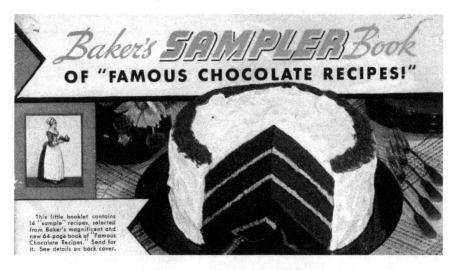

Baker's *Sampler Book* was a small, twelve-page recipe booklet that featured a chocolate layer cake frosted with vanilla chocolate frosting and grated chocolate.

THE BAKER, PIERCE AND FORBES FAMILIES

The Baker family of Dorchester, Massachusetts, was prominent since their arrival in 1635 on the ship *Bachelor*, which brought a group of Puritans from England seeking religious freedom. The immigrant ancestor was Richard Baker, who served as a master's mate, or second man in command. Baker settled on Savin Hill (referred to as "Rock Hill" in the seventeenth century) in Dorchester and joined the Dorchester Meeting House. In 1639, he married Faith Withington, daughter of Henry Withington, who was the ruling elder of Dorchester, an important and respected position in the community. The Bakers were equally well connected; Richard's his brother-in-law was Governor Thomas Danforth of the Massachusetts Bay Colony, and his brothers were a tide mill owner and a merchant. Richard Baker was prominent in the town, serving in various capacities, including selectman, and he was made a freeman of the colony in 1642. He was also a member of the Ancient and Honorable Artillery Company. Baker owned extensive tracts of land at Savin Hill, as well as in the Great Lots, which were owned by his descendants into the nineteenth century. The Baker family retained their Dorchester connections well into the mid-twentieth century, and the descent from Richard Baker, the immigrant ancestor, is as follows (owners of the Baker Chocolate mill are highlighted in **bold**):

Richard Baker (1614–1689) m. Faith Withington (1616–1689)
John Baker (1643–1690) m. Preserved Trott (died 1711)
John Baker (1671–1746) m. Hannah Withington (1686–1768)
James Baker (1713–1776) m. Priscilla Paul (1718–1750)
Dr. James Baker (1739–1825) m. Lydia Bowman (1741–1816)
Edmund Baker (1770–1846) m. Sarah Howe (1771–1802) and Elizabeth Vose Lillie (1767–1843) [Elizabeth and her first husband, John Lillie, were grandparents of **Henry Lillie Pierce**.]
Walter Baker (1792–1852) m. Deborah Smith Mott (1798–1838) and Eleanor Jameson Williams (1806–1891)
Walter Baker Jr. (1827–1887) m. Frances Cordelia Tremlett

Dr. James Baker

James Baker (1739–1825) was the son of James and Priscilla Paul Baker, who lived on the Upper Road (now Washington Street) at Melville Avenue

"Her Favorite Doll" was a charming 1916 advertisement from *Liberty* by Walter Baker & Company, Ltd., that had this adorable child saying, "Now I have my dolly; pretty soon I'll have my cocoa." Who would deny this adorable child Baker's Cocoa?

in Dorchester, Massachusetts. He was educated at the North School. He graduated from Harvard College in 1760 and studied theology with the Reverend Jonathan Bowman (1703–1775), minister of the Dorchester Meeting House for forty-three years. Though he married Lydia Bowman (1741–1816), daughter of the Reverend Jonathan Bowman (their children were Edmund, Elizabeth and Lydia Baker), he left his ministerial studies with her father and began the study of medicine. To support himself and his growing family, he taught school in Dorchester while studying medicine, but by 1762, he was keeping a general store at Dr. Baker's Corner (since 1847 known as Codman Square) at the present corner of Washington Street and Talbot Avenue.

In 1764, Dr. Baker, who would use his medical title for the remainder of his life, met and financially assisted John Hannon in setting up a chocolate mill in a rented mill on the Milton side of the Neponset River at Milton Village. Hannon was adept and skilled as a chocolate maker, having learned the trade in England. Backed by Baker, he produced Hannon's Best Chocolate from 1765 to 1779. In 1780, after Hannon disappeared on a supposed trip to the West Indies to procure cacao beans, Baker bought the interest from his widow, Elizabeth Gore Hannon, and commenced the manufacture of chocolate impressed with his name, "Baker." His brother-in-law, Edward Preston, later assisted by Patrick Connor and Richard Clark, made the chocolate.

Dr. Baker continued in the chocolate business, purchasing imported cacao beans from near and far, and was successful enough to build a fashionable house across from his old general store. The house, a five-bay Colonial, was elegantly furnished and included chairs made by Stephen Badlam, a well-known cabinetmaker in Dorchester Lower Mills. He and his wife,

Lydia Bowman Baker, lived a comfortable life, thanks to the chocolate mill on the Neponset River, and in 1791, their son Edmund joined Baker in the chocolate business. In 1804, Dr. Baker retired from the business, and Edmund assumed control.

Edmund Baker

Edmund Baker (1770–1848) was the son of Dr. James and Lydia Bowman Baker. He was first married to Sarah Howe (1771–1802), and they were the parents of Walter, Charles and Horatio Baker. His second wife was Elizabeth Vose Lillie (1767–1848), daughter of Daniel and Patience Smith Vose and the widow of John Lillie. Their children were Edmund James Baker Jr., James Edmund Baker and Lydia Baker Huntoon.

In 1791, Edmund Baker joined his father at the chocolate mill in Lower Mills and assumed full control in 1804 upon his father's retirement. That year, Edmund Baker hired the 1765 mill of Wentworth & Stone, "fit[ting] it up to do an increased amount of work." In 1805, he bought all interest in the Samuel Leeds Mill, but a year later he fitted his first mill with the first tub wheels in the Boston area and produced chocolate, grist and cloth. The diverse business interests of Baker were obvious, as he also invested in a paper mill; however, his chocolate business increased steadily. In 1813, he razed the mill built seven years earlier and erected on its site a three-story granite mill that was forty by forty feet with a two-story ell for the combined purpose of making woolens, satinets and chocolate.

In 1818, Edmund Baker took his eldest son, Walter Baker, into partnership in the chocolate mill and taught him the business. He retired in 1824.

Edmund James Baker

The corner of Washington and Richmond Streets in the Lower Mills has had a somewhat checkered past, serving as the site of the Knights of Columbus, a vacant lot and, most recently, a new office building, but at one time it was the site of the elegant home of Edmund J. Baker Jr. (1804–1890), grandson of Dr. James Baker. Married to Sarah Howard Bowman Sherman (1809–1870), Edmund Baker, the son of Edmund and Elizabeth Vose Lillie Baker, served for over twenty-five years as president and treasurer of the Dorchester Mutual Fire Insurance Company at Port Norfolk. He was also the surveyor/cartographer who drew the 1831 map of Dorchester and Milton. He served

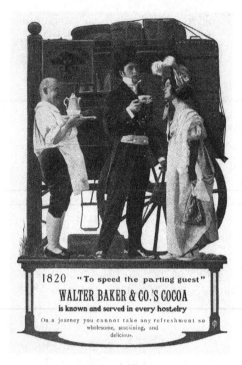

1820 "To speed the parting guest"

WALTER BAKER & CO.'S COCOA

is known and served in every hostelry

On a journey you cannot take any refreshment so
wholesome, sustaining, and
delicious.

It was said in 1820 that Walter Baker & Company's cocoa was "known and served in every hostelry" and that "on a journey you cannot take any refreshment so wholesome, sustaining, and delicious."

as postmaster of Milton and was a major landowner in Dorchester and a noted real estate speculator. At the time of the annexation of Dorchester to the city of Boston on January 4, 1870, he owned Pantheon Hall on Dorchester Avenue, six small houses built for speculation on Dorchester Avenue, ten acres of land near Dorchester Avenue and Adams Street and eight acres of land at Codman Square (the present site of the Lithgow Building, built by the Baker family and designed by local architect Joseph Tilden Greene). A noted genealogist, Baker was also a founder and the second president (1872–1890) of the Dorchester Historical and Antiquarian Society, founded in 1843 and disbanded in 1907; he was a major contributor to the *History of Dorchester* (1859) and the *History of Milton* (1887).

The Lower Mills site was originally the site of Edmund Baker Sr.'s house, a late eighteenth-century house built in 1791 and the family home for over seventy years. However, in 1872, his son Edmund Baker Jr., half brother of Walter Baker, commissioned local architect Charles Austin Wood to build an Italianate mansion, stable and shed on the site of his father's house. Moving the original house to Avondale Street, where it was converted to workers' housing, Wood set about building a commodious house that had numerous reception rooms, a wide wraparound piazza and a cupola from which one could see panoramic views of the Blue Hills. Interestingly, the house was built between two churches: the Methodist-Episcopal Church (now Wesley United Methodist Church) on Washington Street and the Third Religious Society on Richmond Street. The Third Religious Society, formed in 1813, moved its original meetinghouse to Washington Street, where it was converted to Richmond Hall (and where it still stands), and built a larger Greek Revival meetinghouse in 1840, designed by Asher Benjamin. Richmond Street, laid out in 1813, was named for Reverend Richmond, first pastor of the Third Religious Society. As a result, the Baker House was sited between two churches of different denominations, and the property was bounded by a low stonewall on both sides. After Baker's death in 1890, the house was occupied by his daughter, Lydia Bowman Baker Edwards Taft, who left in 1937 for York, Maine, where she died two years later.

Today, the Baker House (demolished in 1937) and the two churches are gone; however, a fairly modern church was built by Wesley United Methodist Church after a disastrous fire in the mid-1960s. The site of the Baker-Edwards House is now the site of a modern office building.

Walter Baker

Walter Baker (1792–1852) was the son of Edmund and Sarah Howe Baker. He graduated from Harvard College in 1811 and then attended Judge Tappan Reeve's Law School in Litchfield, Connecticut. In 1812, he left the law school and returned to Dorchester, where he was engaged in a woolen manufacturing business with five looms during the War of 1812. This business proved immensely successful, as European imports had been curtailed. By 1815, he was in Natchez, Mississippi, teaching school, but three years later he was taken into partnership with his father in the family chocolate mill. In 1824, Walter Baker assumed the presidency of Baker Chocolate upon his father's retirement, and henceforth the company was known as Walter Baker & Company. He married twice. His first wife was Deborah Smith Mott, and they were the parents of Walter Baker Jr. (1825–1887). After her death in 1838, Baker served as chairman of the committee that built Lyceum Hall on Meeting House Hill in Dorchester, an elegant Greek Revival building that served as a place for lectures, dances and community events. His second wife was Eleanor Jameson Williams (1806–1892), whose father was a wealthy Boston East India merchant then living in Philadelphia. They had four children, none of whom survived infancy.

Baker served as colonel of the First Regiment, First Brigade, First Division, of the state militia and was to be known as Colonel Baker for the remainder of his life. However, he devoted himself to the chocolate mill and began an expansion that continued unabated for the next twenty-five years. He introduced a less expensive chocolate known as Lapham, which he named for his employee Elisha Lapham. He also introduced spiced cocoa sticks in 1840, homeopathic chocolate in 1844, J.G. French's Chocolate (named for Baker's coachman Jacob G. French), Caracas chocolate in 1849 and

A trade card of Baker's Cocoa, Chocolate and Broma not only listed the many awards and medals received for the quality of the product but also boasted that "cocoa and chocolates are greatly superior to tea or coffee in all the properties which produce a healthy state of the body, and consequently of the mind."

German's Sweet Chocolate (perfected by Baker's former coachman Samuel German) in 1852. He shipped his chocolate, cocoa and broma throughout the United States, and it was said that Abraham Lincoln and his partner, William Barry, sold Baker's Chocolate and Cocoa in their New Salem, Illinois general store, the only packaged and branded food product available there. In 1834, Baker hired the first two women to work at the mill, sisters Christina and Mary Shields, to wrap and prepare the 750 pounds of chocolate produced daily.

In 1848, the mill built in 1813 by his father, Edmund Baker, was destroyed by fire and was replaced by a new three-story mill designed by Gridley J. Fox Bryant and built of rough-hewn Quincy granite. The mill was impressive and insured for $7,023, with the machinery, pans and utensils being insured for an additional $6,010. A sign bearing the legend "W. Baker & Co., Established 1780" was hung on the façade. This obviously fireproof mill had brick floors, granite walls and a "safe stove" where cocoa was made, and according to *A Calendar of Walter Baker & Company*, it "prevent[ed] incendiaries making their way into the mill...inside shutters [were installed] on all lower story windows."

This new mill was the center of chocolate production, with two men, two apprentices, six girls and a forelady.

Upon his death in 1852, Walter Baker left a chocolate mill that was one of four in the Lower Mills. The aspect of so much chocolate being produced led to the area being known as Chocolate Village, and his family's delicious vision was continued by trustees.

Employees and Associates

Eleanor J.W. Baker

Eleanor Jameson Williams Baker (1806–1891) was the second wife of Walter Baker and a well-known resident of Dorchester during the nineteenth century. Born in Boston on Fort Hill, she was the daughter of Robert Williams, a China trade merchant on Long Wharf in Boston. The Williamses were a well to do family, with Mr. Williams serving as a selectman of Boston and treasurer of the Society of the Cincinnati.

The Bakers were married in 1840 and lived first on Summer Street in Boston. Walter Baker purchased the former Oliver Estate on Washington Street, at the corner of Park Street (present site of the Lucy Stone School), as a summer house. The property was within driving distance of the mill on the Neponset River and afforded a secluded and panoramic building site. The Bakers were the parents of four children, none of whom survived infancy.

After the death of her husband, Mrs. Baker made her permanent home in Dorchester. She was a member of the Second Church of Dorchester at Codman Square, contributing large sums of money over the years. Her husband had donated the four-sided tower clock in 1852. It was in these years that she invited to her home world travelers, well-known guests and cultivated personages. In an undated newspaper clipping, it was said that

The Pierce Mill (left) and the old wood Ware Mill straddle both sides of the Neponset River in the late nineteenth century. In 1902, the Ware Mill was designed by Winslow & Bigelow and replaced the wood mill on the right.

Mrs. Baker "drew to herself a large number of friends in such a hospitable manner that she was never at a loss for companions all the rest of her life. It was commented in her obituary that 'she had a strong character, an independent mind, a discriminating judgment and a boundless charity.'" Indeed, after her husband's death, she was more than comfortable in her circumstances and began to devote a great deal of time and money to worthy charities.

When the Civil War broke out, Mrs. Baker opened her home to Dorchester women, providing large quantities of linens and cotton material to supply the army hospitals. Donating a dining tablecloth a century old, she also gave freely of her fortune. She single-handedly headed the Dorchester women who gathered numerous books and pamphlets for the Soldiers Free Library, a new establishment in Washington, D.C., opened by Elida Rumsey and John A. Fowle, who were later married in the United States House of Representatives. Her wealth also allowed her to travel extensively when it was not a common occurrence to cross the Atlantic Ocean. She was charitable to those who made her acquaintance in Europe. During one of her journeys in Europe, on her return from the Holy Land, she met Dr. Samuel Gridley Howe (of the Perkins Institute for the Blind) in Athens and assisted him

A trade card of "Fruits and their Blossoms" shows grapes and pears as an advertisement of Walter Baker & Company, Ltd. These trade cards had fanciful and often artistic scenes advertising Baker's products.

and his daughter in distributing the garments collected in Boston among the Cretan refugees on the Island of Egina. Indeed, she had a somewhat continental benevolence and traveled far from Dorchester when not doing good works locally.

The Baker House, originally built by Lieutenant Governor Oliver prior to the American Revolution, was a large and imposing Georgian mansion facing Washington Street, with incredible views from the rear of Dorchester Bay and the Harbor Islands. The grounds extended down the hill to what is now Dorchester Avenue and were extended tracts of open land. The house had once been owned by the Honorable Benjamin Hitchborn, who entertained Presidents Jefferson and Madison in his home and also allowed the Dorchester Academy to use one of the rooms for its first school. The house attracted rich and poor, old and young, and it seemed that the only prerequisite for an invitation from Mrs. Baker was a sensible wit and proper manners. When Eleanor Baker died in 1891, her estate was considerable, and she remembered many of her friends, her church and her numerous charities. The mansion became the Colonial Club of Dorchester, a quasi country club that remained until just before World War I, though most of the land had been sold for speculative purposes, with Regina Road, Tremlett and Waldeck Streets, Wellesley Park and Upland Avenue being laid out. Mrs. Baker was a true soldier in her extensive benevolent works.

J. FRANK HOWLAND

Joseph Francis Howland (1845–1919) was born in New Bedford, Massachusetts, the son of Frederick P. Howland and Sarah Slade Marvel Howland. He and his wife, Helen Delano Howland (1848–1915), lived at 690 Adams Street in Dorchester, Massachusetts. After living in California in 1861, he returned to Boston, where he was employed in the Boston office of Baker Chocolate in 1863. According to *The American Series of Popular Biographies* (1891):

> *assiduity with which he discharged his duties and his readiness in learning the details of the business soon won the confidence and strong personal regard of the Hon. Henry L. Pierce, the owner and manager of the works. Mr. Pierce was often absent from his office for long periods during his frequent visits to Europe and while discharging his duties in the various positions to which he was elected in the city, State, and national governments; and during those absences Mr. Howland was entrusted not only with discretion*

of the great and constantly growing business of the Walter Baker Company, but with Mr. Pierce's personal financial affairs.

In 1895, the year the chocolate company was incorporated as Walter Baker & Company, Ltd., Howland was elected the first president and general manager. He served until Pierce's death and the purchase of the company by the Forbes Syndicate.

During his unbroken service of thirty-six years the business has steadily increased until the comparatively small concern of 1863 has come to be the largest establishment of its kind on this continent. It is not too much to say that this remarkable result is due in large measure to the intelligent, conscientious, and unremitting labors of Mr. Howland.

Howland had often been urged to accept nominations or appointments to state and city offices; however, with the exception of two years' service on the Boston City Council (1882–1883), he had always declined public office. In the way of business, he served several years as director of the Laurel Lake Mills, Fall River; director of the Blue Hill National Bank of Milton; and as one of the trustees of Cedar Grove Cemetery, where he and his family are interred.

J. MURRAY FORBES

James Murray Forbes (1845–1937) was the son of Captain Robert Bennet Forbes and Rose Smith Forbes. He followed in his father's footsteps and became a prosperous China trade merchant. Educated in Concord, Massachusetts, he went to China in 1863 at the age of eighteen and spent the next decade there, working for Russell & Company. The Forbes family amassed a huge fortune in the China trade, initially trading North American furs and manufactured goods for tea and other goods from China, but they made a considerable fortune smuggling opium during the Opium Wars. The British wanted to maintain a monopoly on supplying the Chinese with opium produced in India; however, during the Opium Wars, the British ships were prevented from delivering their cargoes of opium, and American shipowners, such as the Forbeses, who could sail the final miles made great amounts of money delivering the addictive cargoes for the British. Starting as a clerk with Russell & Company, J. Murray Forbes advanced rapidly in the family firm and, in 1871, returned to the United States a very wealthy man. He married Alice Frances Bowditch (1848–1929), granddaughter of the great navigator Nathaniel Bowditch, and the couple lived at 107 Commonwealth Avenue in the Back Bay of Boston; on an estate on Isleboro, Maine; and, in the spring and fall, at the house built for his grandmother, Margaret Perkins Forbes, on Milton Hill, now known as the Captain Forbes House Museum at 215 Adams Street, Milton.

In 1897, a year after the death of Henry Lillie Pierce, Forbes headed a syndicate of Boston capitalists and businessmen who purchased the ten thousand shares of stock in Walter Baker & Company, Ltd., at $475 per share, or $4,750,000. The Forbes Syndicate implemented a new cooling system and air conditioning, which allowed the production of chocolate in warm weather, and systematically purchased electric- and gasoline-powered delivery trucks to replace the horse-drawn wagons. Advertising and marketing of the chocolate and cocoa were greatly expanded, with full-page color advertisements in nationwide magazines, leading to widespread use of Baker's Chocolate and Cocoa. The Ware Mill, Preston Mill and Forbes Mill were built during this period as well. One major expansion of the business was when a new production facility was opened in 1911 in Montreal, Canada.

H. CLIFFORD GALLAGHER

Hugh Clifford Gallagher (1855–1931) was the son of Hugh and Alice Truman Gallagher, and he was raised in Sackville, New Brunswick. In 1878, he obtained an office position with the Josiah Webb & Company in Milton Village, where "he became thoroughly familiar with manufacturing processes." In 1881, the company was sold to Henry L. Pierce and incorporated into his burgeoning chocolate empire. Gallagher became superintendant under Pierce until 1896, when he became vice-president in charge of manufacturing. In 1903, he became president of Walter Baker & Company, Ltd. He served in that capacity until 1926, when he was elected chairman of the board.

Gallagher and his wife, Edith Warren Everett Gallagher, initially lived in the former home of Dr. Jonathan Ware and, later, on Russell Street. They later bought the former Peter McIntyre Farm on Hillside Street in the Scotts Woods neighborhood in Milton, where they built a home called Notlim Farm, "Milton" in reverse.

Gallagher served as the Republican delegate from Massachusetts to the 1908 and 1912 Republican National Conventions, as well as on the Milton School Committee. He served as the first president of the Milton Savings Bank and as a trustee of Boston University and Smith College.

As a tribute in the May 9, 1931 edition of the *Milton Record* noted, "Under Mr. Gallagher's presidency, relations of management and operating forces have been harmonious. The employees have been loyal and contented."

WILLIAM B. THURBER

William B. Thurber (1867–1937) was the son of James Danforth and Mary Ann Bartlett Thurber. He was raised and educated in Plymouth, Massachusetts. He graduated from the Massachusetts Institute of Technology in 1889 and served as a trustee and treasurer of the college from 1909 to 1913. He was also a member of the alumni committee. He initially worked for the New England Telephone & Telegraph Company, but in 1898 he was hired as superintendant at Walter Baker & Company.

Thurber served as president of Walter Baker & Company, Ltd., from 1926 to 1938, later serving as chairman of the board of directors. He supported a number of charities in Milton, among them the Milton School Committee; he was president of the Milton Hospital, chair of the Milton Red Cross, treasurer of Milton Academy and vice-president of the Blue Hill Bank & Trust Company.

Only one year after he assumed the presidency of Baker's, it was sold to Postum Cereal Company, later to be known as the General Foods Corporation, for $11 million. As a result, Baker Chocolate became part of a larger consortium of food brands owned by Postum, including Maxwell House coffee and Jell-O gelatin. In 1929, Postum Cereal Company changed its corporate name to General Foods.

Operations of Walter Baker & Company continued under the Postum Company, Inc., a division of General Foods. Partially as a result of acquisition by General Foods, Baker's line of confectionary chocolate expanded. Baker's first milk chocolate was introduced in late 1928.

CURTIS H. GAGER

Curtis Gager served as president of Walter Baker & Company, Ltd. (and as vice-president of General Foods) from 1938 to 1954, a time of tremendous change and innovation in the chocolate industry. The workforce during his tenure was the largest in the history of the company, with three shifts of eight hours on a daily basis.

Chocolate "babs," or small rectangles of chocolate, were patented by Curtis H. Gager in 1936 and were made as one-ounce squares of chocolate, with "each square conveniently divided into half-ounce pieces."

Curtis H. Gager (1901–1962) was born in Wilkes Barre, Pennsylvania, the son of Elmer Prosper and Minnie Harrison Gager. He was hired by General Foods and worked at the Baker Division as early as 1935, when he filed a patent with the United States Patent Office. The patent was issued in March 1936. He had submitted a "Design for a Chocolate Bab," a divisible chocolate tablet that made using pieces of a chocolate bar easier. This patent was issued as Patent# D 988858 and was immediately implemented by the chocolate production division. It is still in use today, with each bab, or square, of chocolate embossed with a profile of the trademark.

After Gager, who was affectionately known as "Curbs" Gager, left Baker Chocolate, he became a business advisor and management consultant in New York City. He served as vice-president in charge of sales at the Coca-Cola Company and, later, as the head of Interpublic, the parent company of the advertising agency McCann-Erickson Inc.

The closing of the Dorchester mills of the Baker production facility with the move to Dover, Delaware, in 1965 was a huge employment loss locally. The only division to remain was the "Dream Whip" division, but that, too, was moved in 1969. Phillip Morris Companies acquired General Foods in 1985 and Kraft, Inc., in 1988. Phillip Morris merged the two to form Kraft General Foods in 1989 and subsequently renamed the company Kraft Foods in 1995. Today, Baker's remains a division of Kraft Foods, and after many years of production in Dover, Delaware, Baker's Chocolate is produced for Kraft Foods by a comanufacturer at a facility in Quebec.

After 1965, the mills along the Neponset River were not fully used and had a precarious existence until the early 1980s, when the Commonwealth of Massachusetts Department of Environmental Management acquired the Administration Building for use as a proposed visitor's center for a heritage state park. The center never came to fruition. The building remained vacant until it was developed by Keen Development Corporation and renovated and restored into 13 affordable artist studios and living spaces. Keen Development and Keefe Companies renovated and adapted the Pierce Mill, with the Boston Architectural Team, for 133 apartment rentals, and the Forbes Mill and the Park Mill were adapted for luxury condominiums.

CHOCOLATE VILLAGE

Fourteen Acres of Floor Space
Producing Chocolate

Located on the Neponset River, the Lower Mills and Milton Village are only five miles from Five Corners, today referred to as Edward Everett Square, which borders Roxbury and South Boston, the original settlement area of Dorchester. Milton Village was the site of the town's first gristmill, built in 1634, when Israel Stoughton was granted permission by the Great and General Court to erect a water-powered mill. Within a few decades, with the harnessing of water power through a dam, the Lower Mills had the first gunpowder mill, the first paper mill, the first chocolate mill and the first playing card manufactory in the United States, as well as a thriving mill village on both sides of the Neponset River.

The Lower Mills is the junction of Dorchester Avenue and Adams and Washington Streets and is now known as Pierce Square in memory of Henry Lillie Pierce, one-time president of the Baker Chocolate Company, former mayor of the city of Boston and a United States congressman. The area was known as "Unquety" by its original inhabitants, the Neponset tribe of the Massachusetts Indians. The name "Unquety" referred to the lower falls, or the "Unquetyquisset," at present-day Mattapan. Though all of these names apply to the Lower Mills, the Puritans who settled Dorchester and their descendants referred to this area as "Neponset" until 1832, when the neighborhood in Dorchester stretching from Pope's Hill to Quincy was so named.

Though Dorchester's population was widespread and never exceeded eight thousand until the years after the Civil War, the Lower Mills was an area where many people lived in proximity to their place of employment. Not only were the Upper Road (Washington Street) and the Lower Road (Adams Street) thoroughfares that led directly to the Lower Mills, but the Dorchester Turnpike (now Dorchester Avenue) was also laid out in 1805 to connect the industrial concerns in the Lower Mills with Boston. The Dorchester Turnpike was a straight and fairly level toll road, with a fee per weight if one's cart carried supplies to or from the Lower Mills. As the two other streets were "free streets," Yankee frugality ruled and the toll road failed.

During the period from 1830 to 1860, the "mill village" concept of the Lower Mills began to change as large numbers of millworkers began moving to the area in search of employment. These workers, mostly Western Europeans, came from many different religious groups and countries, and they founded numerous churches, diversifying the religious mix of the area. By the time of the Civil War, churches that embraced Methodist-Episcopalians, Episcopalians, Baptists and Roman Catholics joined the Congregational and Unitarian faiths, and the spectrum of European countries represented was even more diverse.

The Lower Mills is a fine example of a mill village, where nineteenth-century mills survive beside workers' row housing, mill managers' housing and residential districts. This area grew tremendously from 1765, when Dr. James Baker and John Hannon began the production of chocolate in a rented mill on the Milton side of the Neponset River, into a mill complex of substantial buildings at the turn of the twentieth century, most of which were designed by Nathaniel Jeremiah Bradlee and his successors, Winslow and Wetherell.

The following is a list of the important Baker Chocolate mill buildings in the Dorchester Lower Mills and Milton Village. They are not arranged chronologically.

WEBB MILL (BRADLEE & WINSLOW, 1882)
1 Eliot Street, Milton Village

The Webb Mill was named for the Webb Chocolate Company (1843–81), formerly known as the Webb & Twombley Chocolate Company, which was founded by Josiah Webb and Josiah Twombley. Henry Lillie Pierce built the mill a year after he purchased the competitor's company and subsequently named it for the former chocolate and cocoa manufacturer. The mill was designed in the Romanesque Revival style, with red brick and rough-hewn brownstone as corner and detail work. The use of large arches for both window surrounds and an entrance drive to a loading dock makes this mill a dramatic architectural contrast to the Pierce Mill just across the street. With a staggered brick cornice and superb hand-wrought iron gates to the entrance drive, the Webb Mill epitomizes the use of the Romanesque style in Boston.

The Webb Mill is in Milton Village at the corner of Adams and Eliot Streets, just south of the Neponset River. Street traffic includes horse-drawn carriages and wagons, as well as numerous pedestrians.

On the far right is a one-story office projecting over the Neponset River, and in the rear are remnants of the original Webb Chocolate Mill. Today, there are small professional offices in the upper floors, and on the first two floors is the Milton Hill Health Club.

BAKER MILL (WINSLOW & WETHERELL, 1895)
1245 Adams Street, Dorchester Lower Mills

Named for Walter Baker and the three generations of his family that founded and operated the company from 1765 until 1852, the Baker Mill was built on the site of the stone mill of 1813, which was rebuilt in fireproof Quincy granite in 1848 following a fire and was often referred to as the "Old Stone Mill." The Baker Mill is a classically designed Romanesque Revival mill with massive arches joining four stories. With an arched cornice, the red brick mill has quoining and large windows with brick detailing. There is a recessed copper, pressed sheath connector between the Baker Mill and the Forbes Mill. This mill has recently been converted by Keen Associates into attractive apartments, known as the Lofts at Lower Mills and marketed as a WinnResidential Community.

THE POWER HOUSE (WINSLOW & BIGELOW, 1906)
Rear of the Webb Building, Milton Village

A two-hundred-foot smokestack rises high above the powerhouse and mill complex, making it one of the more readily identifiable parts of the mill complex. This Classical, red brick, four-story building with Romanesque detail was built as the electrical power station for the Baker Chocolate complex. Electricity for lights and motors replaced the earlier steam engines and allowed for the installation of a much-needed refrigeration plant, with three boilers and two generators that allowed for the production of chocolate throughout the year. Due to chocolate's low melting point, production had often been suspended during the hot summer months before the erection of the powerhouse.

THE FORBES MILL AND PARK MILL BUILDING
(WINSLOW & WETHERELL, 1911)
1235–1241 Adams Street, Dorchester Lower Mills

Built two decades after the Baker Mill, the Forbes Mill is an almost exact replica in scale, detailing and materials of the earlier mill. The mill was named for the Forbes Syndicate. J. Murray Forbes (1845–1937), of Milton and Boston's Back Bay, headed a syndicate of investors in the purchase of the Baker Chocolate Company in 1897 after Henry Lillie Pierce's death the previous year. Forbes lived near the mill complex, with an "in between" spring and autumn house located at 215 Adams Street on Milton Hill. The Forbes estate is now known as the Captain Robert Bennet Forbes House, a Greek Revival house designed by Isaiah Rogers (1800–1869) for Sarah Perkins Forbes, mother of the successful China trade merchant, and in memory of his brother, Thomas Tunno Forbes, who died in a typhoon in China.

Above: The Baker Mill (left) and the Forbes Mill were designed by Winslow & Wetherell and built in 1895 and 1911, respectively. Adams Street, seen in the foreground, was lined with mills by the turn of the twentieth century.

Left: Looking east on the Neponset River, the power plant and the Baker Mill are on the Boston side of the river. For over a century, water power was used to power the mill on the Neponset River, but by 1900 the mills were powered by steam and, later, electricity.

The Park Mill, which is directly behind the Forbes Mill, was built in 1928 by General Foods Corporation as a machine shop and a storehouse and is distinguished by its bold Art Deco style, using red brick and concrete detailing, with huge banks of wide, multipaned windows.

Both the Forbes Mill and the Park Mill have been converted into luxury condominiums and provide homes for condo owners in the former chocolate mills. The Park Mill also offers a swimming pool and a weight and exercise room.

THE ADMINISTRATION BUILDING
(GEORGE F. SHEPARD JR., 1919)
1205 Adams Street, Dorchester Lower Mills

Built to house the executive offices and a small museum and exhibition room on the history of chocolate and the Baker Chocolate Company, the Administration Building has a monumental Ionic portico and a balustrade along the roof lines. It is prominently sited on a knoll overlooking Adams Street and can be seen from all the mill buildings, as well as by pedestrians and motorists in the Lower Mills. Milton resident and architect George F. Shepard Jr. of the Boston architectural firm of Shepard & Stearns designed this classical Georgian Revival building, the first instance of a building in the Baker mill complex not designed by Bradlee, Winslow & Wetherell. The grandess of the design was embellished by a large neon sign, which illuminated the Lower Mills with "Walter Baker" until 1966 and remains in place on the roof, but without its neon lights. The interior is of an impressive Classical style, with a sweeping marble staircase that rises to meet a life-sized reproduction of *La Belle Chocolatiere*, adopted as the trademark of the Baker Chocolate Company in 1883.

THE STOREHOUSES
(ARCHITECT UNKNOWN, 1888–1890)
Adams Street, South of the Pierce and
Ware Mills, Milton Village

The two storehouses on the south bank of the Neponset River are simple in form and design, especially in regards to their intended use. These red brick storehouses had wood docks that enabled the workmen to load horse-drawn wagons, and later diesel trucks, with wrapped and boxed chocolates

The balustrades of the Administration Building swirl up the staircase and the balcony above as two men converse opposite a copy of *Das Schokoladenmadchen*, which was renamed *La Belle Chocolatiere* by Henry Lillie Pierce. This painting was done by Howard B. Smith and placed in a position of honor at the top of the staircase. *Courtesy of Jane Schroth Lemire.*

The east side of Adams Street in 1905 had, from the left, the Adams, Pierce and Preston Mills and the Ware Mill on the south side of the Neponset River.

and cocoa that were then delivered throughout Boston or shipped by railroad. The storehouses were built in the late 1880s, utilizing both the Queen Anne and Romanesque Revival styles. Well sited, the storehouses were adjacent to the Dorchester and Milton Branch of the Old Colony Railroad, later the surface trolley connecting Mattapan to Ashmont Station on the Red Line. Today, the usage of the storehouses is being debated, and it is hoped that they will become an integral part of the Lower Mills/ Milton Village revitalization.

THE PIERCE MILL (BRADLEE & WINSLOW, 1872)
1220–1222 Adams Street, Dorchester Lower Mills

The Pierce Mill was built two years after Dorchester was annexed to the city of Boston and while Pierce was the mayor of Boston. It is an impressive French Second Empire design that uses red brick, with arched windows, contrasting window lintels and a heavily bracketed cornice. Its size and scale were dramatic and made quite an impression, ensuring the prominence of the Baker Chocolate Company as a leading producer of chocolate in the United States.

Named for Henry Lillie Pierce (1825–1896), president of the company from 1854 until his death, the Pierce Mill was the first structure he had built to allow for the expansion of the production of chocolate and cocoa. Not only did Pierce have his office here, in the projecting wing on the right overlooking the Neponset River, but also chocolate was produced and wrapped in this building. The mill has pedimented gables and brick stringcourses that carry one's eye across the façade, while the use of a mansard roof, which retains its cast-iron cresting, as well as the use of its sloping site, creates additional importance. Today, the Pierce Mill has been converted to attractive affordable apartments by the Boston Architectural Team and Keen Development Corporation. The mill restoration was honored with a Preservation Award from the Massachusetts Historical Commission in 1986, the Victorian Society, New England Chapter, and a twenty-fifth-anniversary National Award from the Advisory Council on Historic Preservation in 1988.

THE WARE MILL (WINSLOW & BIGELOW, 1902)
South of the Pierce Mill, Adams Street, Milton Village

The Ware Mill was named after former chocolate manufacturer Dr. Jonathan Ware (1797–1877), a well-respected physician in Milton and somewhat of a well-known wit who often said, "Well, if people would only rest, there wouldn't be occasion to take so much medicine!" The mill is an elegant, classical Georgian Revival red brick building on the site of Dr. Ware's Chocolate Company. This former competitor of Baker's was purchased by Henry Lillie Pierce, who had a classically detailed mill with quoining, dentilled cornice and keystones above the window lintels. The mill is presently being rehabilitated for condos, and a codfish weather vane soars high above the building. Dr. Ware erected a chocolate mill with two reaction wheels in 1840; it was then leased to Josiah Webb and Josiah F. Twombley in 1843, and they commenced the manufacture of chocolate and cocoa. Adjacent to the Ware Mill is a three-story wood-shingled building at the edge of the Neponset River that survives from the original Dr. Ware Mill, built in 1840.

THE PRESTON MILL (WINSLOW & BIGELOW, 1903)
Rear of the Pierce Mill, Adjacent to the Ware Mill,
Dorchester Lower Mills

The red brick Preston Mill was named for Edward Preston (1744–1819), brother-in-law of Dr. James Baker. The Preston Mill uses similar architectural details as the Ware Mill, except for a more heavily dentilled cornice. The

Pierce Square in the Dorchester Lower Mills was named for Henry Lillie Pierce, who transformed the Baker company from a single mill to a complex and increased the chocolate business fortyfold by the time of his death. Streetcars brought workers to the mills, and shops lined the streets to cater to the many employees.

The Adams Mill, designed by Winslow & Wetherell and built in 1888–89, follows the curve of Adams Street as it turns into Pierce Square.

Preston Chocolate Company was a friendly competitor of Baker Chocolate until it was sold by the Preston heirs in 1859 to Henry D. Chapin, who in turn sold it to Henry Lillie Pierce a year later. The Preston Mill has been converted to attractive apartments.

THE ADAMS STREET MILL
(WINSLOW & WETHERELL, 1888–1889)
1200 Adams Street, Dorchester Lower Mills

The Adams Street Mill was named for Adams Street, known as the "Lower Road," which connected Meeting House Hill with the Lower Mills. In 1840, it was renamed in honor of John Adams (1735–1826), second president of the United States and Adams Street resident. Built in the Romanesque Revival style in red brick, the mill was designed with a gentle rounded curve conforming to the configuration of Adams Street as it bends to enter the Lower Mills. Large arched windows and arched brick corbelling at the cornice make for a dramatic façade. The six-story mill is one of the more simply detailed structures in the mill complex, but its situation is impressive. The arched connector that joins this mill with the Pierce Mill spans the entrance to a cobblestone-paved courtyard that was once a loading area. Here, cacao beans would arrive in large burlap bags and leave as neatly wrapped bars of Baker's Chocolate. Today, the courtyard is the entrance to the apartments in the Pierce, Ware and Preston Mills.

BAKER WAREHOUSE (GEORGE F. SHEPARD JR., 1947)
4 River Street, Dorchester Lower Mills

The warehouse at the corner of Washington and River Streets was built in 1947 for Walter Baker & Company, a division of General Foods, as a shipping and receiving warehouse with a loading dock. The modern-designed, red brick, one-story building was located near the sixteen cocoa bean storage silos that were adjacent to the railroad spur of the New Haven Railroad. The warehouse—designed by noted Milton architect George F. Shepard Jr. of the Boston architectural firm Shepard & Stearns, which also designed the Baker Administration Building on Adams Street—was built by Walter Kidde Constructors, Inc., an innovative modern industrial builder based in New York City. The basement had space for the storage of cocoa, and the first floor was a combination of storage, assembly, shipping docks and office space. The warehouse was sold in 1965, upon the wholesale move of the Walter Baker & Company to Dover, Delaware, to Burke Warehouse, Inc., for use as a warehouse and office. The former warehouse was recently renovated by Shaw's Supermarket as a neighborhood market.

BIBLIOGRAPHY

American Series of Popular Biographies. Massachusetts Edition. Boston: Graves & Steinbarger, 1891. [This volume contains biographical sketches of representative citizens of the commonwealth of Massachusetts.]

Baker, Edmund J., comp. *New England Historical and Genealogical Register*. Vol. XLIII, *Genealogy of Richard Baker*. Boston: New England Historic Genealogical Society, 1889.

Buchanan, Paul, and Anthony Sammarco. *Milton*. Dover, NH: Arcadia Publishing, 1996.

———. *Milton Architecture*. Dover, NH: Arcadia Publishing, 2000.

Bugbee, James M. *Cocoa and Chocolate: A Short History of Their Production and Use*. Dorchester, MA: Walter Baker & Company, Ltd., 1886.

Chapple, Joe Mitchell. "The House That Baker Built." *National Magazine* (June 1906).

Dorchester Community News, 1986–1993.

Hamilton, Edward Pierce. *Chocolate Village*. Milton Historical Society, January 1966.

Miller, Bruce, ed. *A Calendar of Walter Baker & Company, Inc. and Its Times (1765–1940)*. New York: General Foods Corporation, 1940.

Milton Record, 1885–1960.

Orcutt, William Dana. *Good Old Dorchester: A Narrative History of the Town, 1630–1893*. Cambridge, MA: Published by the author, J. Wilson & Son, University Press, 1893.

Sammarco, Anthony Mitchell. *Dorchester*. Dover, NH: Arcadia Publishing, 1995.

———. *Dorchester*. Vol. II. Dover, NH: Arcadia Publishing, 2000.

———. *Dorchester Then & Now*. Dover, NH: Arcadia Publishing, 2005.

BIBLIOGRAPHY

————. *Milton Then & Now*. Dover, NH: Arcadia Publishing, 2004.

Teele, Albert K. *The History of Milton, Massachusetts 1640–1887*. Boston: Press of Rockwell & Churchill, 1887.

Walter Baker & Company. *The Chocolate-Plant and Its Products*. Dorchester, MA: Walter Baker and Company, Ltd., 1891.

————. *Description of the Educational Exhibit of Cocoa and Chocolate*. Dorchester, MA: Walter Baker & Company, Ltd., 1923.